"This is a full-throttle, working-class, single-mother, progressive, hard-drinking, feminist series of essays/meditations/rants on where America and the author's life are headed as the midwestern homemade Trump signs blur past. Go along for the ride—if you dare. You won't regret it."

—SUE WILLIAM SILVERMAN, author of *Acetylene Torch Songs: Writing True Stories to Ignite the Soul*

"In *Thank You for Staying with Me* Bailey Gaylin Moore restlessly and ingeniously proves that a dedicated engagement of home becomes—as we age and evolve—in turns an act of redefinition and refusal, of dismantling and reconsecration. Such acts, in this brilliant essay collection, carry with them a narrative vulnerability that is as electric as it is raw, as it is exhilaratingly curious, filtering intense formative experience through inquiries into psycholinguistics, the behavior of the cosmos, legislative policymaking, philosophy, symbology, entropy, and more. Such ruminations gather an uncommon gravity as they twine to become one of the more earth-shattering comments on family that I've ever read. These essays—and their urgent drive to make sense of the human experience in both macro and micro ways—stand not only as testaments to but also as demonstrations of love."

—MATTHEW GAVIN FRANK, author of *Flight of the Diamond Smugglers*

"We read to understand the world and ourselves a little better. To enter the mind and heart of another through the power of words. To feel seen. In *Thank You for Staying with Me* Bailey Gaylin Moore gives us just that. A writer of tremendous candor, tenderness, and empathy, Moore provides an intelligent, deeply moving account of loss, trauma, depression, and teen motherhood. . . . Formally inventive and brilliantly written, these essays are both enlightening and emotionally evocative. Her impressive knowledge and background in philosophy, ontology, culture, and politics provide thoughtful context and complexity to these works as well. In the end, though, this is a book about healing and grace, hope and transcendence. The complicated love for an imperfect place and its people. And the debt of gratitude we owe the ones who stay with us."

—KATHY FISH, author of *Wild Life: Collected Works, 2003-2018*

"*Thank You for Staying with Me* isn't just a great book; it is a necessary one. Bailey Gaylin Moore's writing is as powerful as writing the hard truth gets. She grew up in the Ozarks, a conservative part of this country, but what happened to her there could have happened anywhere—and does. I was bowled over by the immediacy of her prose and moved by the magical grace of her blessings. This is astonishing writing."

—ABIGAIL THOMAS, *New York Times* best-selling author of *What Comes Next and How to Like It*

"A breathlessly beautiful, exhilarating collection throbbing with power and life. Bailey Gaylin Moore writes with impressive wit, shattering tenderness, and aching vulnerability. Mother-daughter relationships, selfhood, systemic injustice, and reckoning with the past are all delivered with stunning insight and love. This is a gorgeous, highly recommended collection."

—JENNIFER MARITZA MCCAULEY, author of *When Trying to Return Home*

"In *Thank You for Staying with Me*, Bailey Gaylin Moore offers exegeses of music ('the importance of dissonance'), of history and lore ('the myth of vagina dentata'), and of modern philosophy ('Heidegger's non-choices'), and the hilariously titled section 'Hegel Exercises' through a telling of her personal history in Missouri, in relationships with men, and in academia, using a dizzying blend of comic moments, sober revelations, and urgent lyrical explorations. *Thank You for Staying with Me* is meta, metal, and metaphysical. With a lens that encompasses the astronomical and the microscopic—as well as the human-scaled phenomena of Spencer's Gifts and baseball dads—this book takes the reader on a thrilling journey of the detours and digressions of a mind coming to terms with a world in flux. Treat yourself and read this book."

—PHONG NGUYEN, author of *Bronze Drum* and *Roundabout*

THANK YOU FOR STAYING WITH ME

AMERICAN LIVES
Series editor: Tobias Wolff

Thank You for Staying with Me

Essays

BAILEY GAYLIN MOORE

University of Nebraska Press
LINCOLN

© 2025 by the Board of Regents of the University of Nebraska

Acknowledgments for the use of copyrighted material appear on pages 203–205, which constitute an extension of the copyright page.

All rights reserved

The University of Nebraska Press is part of a land-grant institution with campuses and programs on the past, present, and future homelands of the Pawnee, Ponca, Otoe-Missouria, Omaha, Dakota, Lakota, Kaw, Cheyenne, and Arapaho Peoples, as well as those of the relocated Ho-Chunk, Sac and Fox, and Iowa Peoples.

∞

Library of Congress Cataloging-in-Publication Data

Names: Moore, Bailey Gaylin, author.
Title: Thank you for staying with me: essays / Bailey Gaylin Moore.
Other titles: Thank you for staying with me (Compilation)
Description: Lincoln: University of Nebraska Press, [2025] | Series: American lives
Identifiers: LCCN 2024024808
ISBN 9781496241931 (paperback)
ISBN 9781496242860 (epub)
ISBN 9781496242877 (pdf)
Subjects: LCSH: Moore, Bailey Gaylin, author. | Authors, American—21st century—Biography. | Women authors, American—21st century—Biography. | LCGFT: Autobiographies. | Essays.
Classification: LCC PS3613.O55398 Z46 2025 | DDC 814/.6 [B]—dc23/eng/20240919
LC record available at https://lccn.loc.gov/2024024808

Designed and set in Merope by K. Andresen.

for my mom, son, and all my former selves:

thank you for staying with me

CONTENTS

Author's Note   xi

Step One: How to Be a Daughter   1

Mostly My Mother's Daughter   3

Second Molars   5

Behind the Subway in Chesterfield Village   13

Puke Angels   17

Dark Center of the Universe   19

The End of the Rainbow   33

Choices   41

Step Two: How to Hold a Baby   43

Piece by Piece   45

ACTing   49

Wall of Water   51

Step Three: How to Be a Student   55

Galaxy Identification   57

Hegel Exercises   63

Count the Beats   69

Unbreaking an Egg   75

A Scattering of Our Own   79

Step Four: How to Untangle Knots   91

One Fish, Two Fish   93

Matted and Mangled   99

Life Is Too Short Not to Get Beef Jerky from a Van on the Side of a Highway   101

Dissonance   109

If You Build It, Baseball Dads Will Come   113

Step Five: How to Mourn a Nation   117

Mein(e) C—   119

Reclaiming Voices Like Needles in Haystacks   127

Twitter's Hot Takes on Women in Politics   131

Gal-vanized   139

Step Six: How to Love Your Home   141

Two Degrees of Separation from Brad Pitt   143

When Natalie Walks into the Snow   145

Penumbra   155

D Explains How to Speak to a Police Officer   167

All Things Being Equal   171

Homecoming   175

Overkill   187

Praying to Lyra   189

Brave New World   193

Thank You for Staying with Me   195

Acknowledgments   203

AUTHOR'S NOTE

When I'm overwhelmed with gratitude, I tell someone, "Thank you for Being." Maybe I studied too much Heidegger and ontology—the study of Being—in my undergrad, or perhaps the state of existing and feeling loved causes such warmth that I have to stop and give thanks. These essays explore my own fascination with ontology, language, and the cosmos, and how relationships and place impact the self.

I end up thinking about community, about how every action has consequences, including every inaction. How does that implicate Being for others? And how can we make this a space for fellowship in a time where it feels like, more often than not, there are more harmful decisions we can make when it comes to Being than there are good.

For a long time, I wished I had possessed some kind of step-by-step how-to guide for Being and navigating this world, but I guess the point of all this existential dogshit is to make our own blueprints. This is what writing these essays did for me, and, like everything found within this book, these moments are through my own subjective lens of experience, like everyone else's blueprint.

THANK YOU FOR STAYING WITH ME

Step One

How to Be a Daughter

Be strong-willed to upset your mother, except when she is sad, in which case, rub her back in silence as she stares out the window, like she does to you during the boring parts of Sunday morning service.

Try to run away from home when you are four because your mother and you got in a fight. You didn't want to finish your asparagus. Or perhaps you didn't say *thank you*, even after she tried so hard to instill the importance of showing gratitude. She'll chase you into Roberta Stainback's yard, but you'll tease that you are too quick for her, that you will never come home. In your memory, Roberta Stainback's yard feels miles away, but it's only catty-corner to your own.

Your mother does catch you, and shortly after, Roberta Stainback bought your mother a book on how to raise strong-willed children. Your mother will tell you this as an adult, and you, laughing it off, will ask, "Was I really all that difficult?" You were. And you still are, because even decades later, you're still working toward a proper thank-you to the woman who raised you, who, as everyone reminds you, could be your twin when looking at side-by-side photos, one of you in eighth grade and her in her senior year. Dirty-blonde hair and green eyes. A slightly crooked, shy smile. Skin so light it will explode if exposed under sunbeams for too long.

Perhaps the fact you matured so quickly is why she'll hover over you in your teenage years, worried about every choice you make. At the time, you won't realize why mothers don't want their daughters to grow up too quickly, but like the book Roberta Stainback bought implies: You are a headstrong child.

As an adult, you'll wonder if all daughters are headstrong, or if that's just a word ascribed to strong daughters because the inherent nature of daughterhood is complicating the lives of their mothers.

Mostly My Mother's Daughter

An April Easter, just late enough for the gummy Ozarks' air to cause my ivory tights to stick to babyweighted thighs. I'm five, maybe six. The good years stick together, I'll realize later in life. My father hasn't left my mother, so I haven't seen heartbreak yet, and I won't for a few more years. When I'm eight, heartbreak will look like this for my mother: petting the family shepherd on the stairs and looking out the window. She will try to hide the noise of tears, but I will hear her from my bedroom on the other side of the foyer. I will come out, and she will apologize for her pain. I will take a seat beside her, tell her it's okay. We will sit together in silence.

There's an elephant of a boulder outside the house, the only place I'll ever call home with confidence. My brother and I jump between the front porch and this rock, a cement flower bed lining the deck as your Point A. I follow his lead. He jumps to Point B, and I follow, the two of us are just small enough to land comfortably on the small sedimentary elephant. We both find ourselves back at Point A.

Our mother comes out, ready for Easter service. Hair-teased and shoulder-padded, she looks like a movie star. She sits on the rock watching my brother and me, now traipsing along the cement flower bed. My brother stumbles, falls off into the lake of burgundy foliage.

"Lava," I say. "You fell into the lava."

As an adult, I'll try to remember the name of the burgundy foliage. *Alternanthera*, my mother will tell me. This is too many syllables to be true. Even thirty years later, it will still be lava. This ground, this home, an untouchable place.

While we wait for our father, I hop down into the leafy lava—the "Alternanthera"—to be close to my mother. Later, I will forget what we talked about that Easter morning. It would be the last Easter we went to church together as a family, and perhaps I would have paid more attention to the conversations had I known I'd be rubbing my mom's back as she looked out the window and cried. Perhaps I would have paid less attention to my brother and I jumping from point A to point B on an Easter Sunday had I known he and I would both grow up to be complacently churchless.

It's possible my mother asked me about my future that Sunday morning. Something she did often—her own game.

"What do you want to be when you grow up?"

"A mom," I would say. The answer remained the same until I hit puberty.

She would always question this. "But besides a mom?" she'd asked.

"Just a mom," I said.

I wanted to be just like her, which is confirmed every time she tells the story of me at three-years-old asking if I would have bigger breasts when I grew up. I patted my chest and said, "I want to have big titties just like you!"

I ended up having big titties just like her, but it wasn't something I patted my chest over. Instead, my shame grew along with my cup size. I'd try to press myself down with layered sports bras and tight tank tops to make me look flatter. In middle school, I'd play the role of a jock, hiding underneath loose T-shirts as I inevitably became the woman I always thought I wanted to be.

Second Molars

1.

You look mature for fourteen: high cheekbones, arched brows, classic face muddled from dark makeup. When your older brother's friends smile in your direction, he gives them a steady eye, mouth firm with warning. And when your mother sees men glance in your direction, she reminds you of your age, patting the crown of your dirty-blonde head like she did when she said goodbye on your first day of kindergarten.

Swat her hand away, just as you did on that first day of kindergarten. *It's okay*, you tell her, drawing on thicker eyeliner the next morning to hide your age. Thicker eyeliner to impress older friends, friends like Jillian, cigarette hanging out of her mouth, fists raised against the world. Thicker eyeliner to make boys sitting on high school hallway vents look at you the same way the men your mother warned you about do.

2.

Vagina Dentata, /vəˈdʒaɪnə dɛnˈteɪtə/ [< Latin *dentata*, adj., having teeth, toothed]
    n. (*Cultural Anthropol. and Psychol.*)

    1. A vagina equipped with teeth occurring in myth, folklore, and religion. Vagina Dentata symbolizes fear of castration, the dangers of sexual intercourse, of birth or rebirth, etc. Makes penis either: 1. shrunken, afraid, or 2. altogether obsolete. Additionally, Vagina Dentata gives new meaning to Tupac's words, *I ain't a killer, but don't push me, revenge is the sweetest joy next to getting pussy.*

3.

In 2010, Dr. Sonnet Ehlers created Rape-aXe condoms to combat overwhelming rape statistics in South Africa. The toothed condom will latch onto a future attacker, jagged teeth clenching down harder if he pulls out of his victim. In an interview regarding distributing Rape-aXe condoms throughout the continent, a Ugandan representative for Disease Control and Prevention told CNN, "The fears surrounding the victim, the act of wearing the condom in anticipation of being assaulted all represent enslavement that no woman should be subject to."

And if his intentions are pure, thoughts of Rape-aXe condoms may cause faltering breaths even if she only says, *Well, just the tip*. Momentary in comparison to the indefinite female anticipation, anticipation being the way she gauges potential trust in men she will meet, perhaps in men she may already know — in any man she habitually lowers her head to while passing by on the street. Her history of unnamed enslavement.

4.

Canine, /ˈkeɪnʌɪn/, [< Latin *canīnus*, < *canis* dog]

> n. (*Anat. and Physiol.*)
>
> 1. strong pointed teeth, one situated on each side of the upper and lower jaw between the incisors and the molars. Predatory teeth — teeth to tear food. Teeth to bite back hard
>
> adj.
>
> 1. supposes an appetite, supposes hunger: voracious, greedy, as that of a dog

5.

Branson, Missouri: Jillian buys cigarettes at a gas station with a tourist tax rate. You try a puff while she calls your mother pretending to be a parent chaperone on a trip just far enough from home. You hear her voice on the other end — *Sounds like fun*, she says. You unclench your jaws and breathe in the smoke.

When you return, your mother will ask about all the fun adventures you had: Waltzing Waters, Celebration City, perhaps

Andy Williams singing "Moon River"—performances that will die within a decade. Branson's ghosts will leave behind chipped bright mansions and fallen neon signs, remnants of your childhood calling out in the night.

Instead of watching Andy Williams sing "Moon River," you go to a crusty hotel room off the strip. Jillian invites men who tell you how you look pretty in your red dress, men who ask how old you are, talking with Budweiser cans clutched in too-large hands. You say, *I don't know how old I am*, laughing through gritted teeth.

6.

1926—J. I. Suttie tr. S. Ferenczi *Further Contrib. Psycho-anal.* xxxii. 279. "Anxiety in regard to the mother's vagina (vagina dentata = birth anxiety)."

7.

While Sigmund Freud shifts in his sleep, he dreams of his mother telling him to clean
>   dirty
>   dishes.
He dreams of his mother, a castrated woman, a woman smiling with her front teeth.
Sigmund Freud's mother says, *Do your homework, do your math equations.*
He dreams of his mother, tucking him into bed—tight,
>   safe
He dreams of his mother carrying him with her   hip out,
>   his   father touching the arch
>   of   her   back.
His mother. *All boys dreams of*   their   mother, Sigmund Freud says.
He dreams of his mother, the head of Medusa, laughing—
>   snaked-hair wild, their teeth
>   alive, teeth snapping.

Sigmund Freud dreams of his mother.

8.

Molar, /ˈmoʊlər/, [< classical Latin *molāris* grinding tooth < *mola* millstone]

n. (*Anat. and Physiol.*)

SECOND MOLARS 7

1. each of the grinding teeth at the back of a mammal's mouth, typically having a broad occlusal surface and cusps, crescents, or ridges; a molar tooth, a grinding tooth, a tooth that grinds.

9.

Millstone, /ˈmɪlˌstoʊn/, [Cognate with or formed similarly to West Frisian *molestien*, Middle Dutch *molensteen* (Dutch *molensteen*), Old Saxon *mulinstēn* (Middle Low German *mölenstēn*), Old High German *mulinstein*, *mülstein* (Middle High German *mülstein*, German *Mühlstein*), Norwegian (Bokmål) *møllestein*, Danish *møllesten* <the Germanic base of mill n.1 + the Germanic base of stone n.]

n. (*agricult.*)

1. Either of a pair of circular stones which grind corn by the rotation of the upper stone on the lower (or nether) one.

n. (*fig.*)

1. A heavy and inescapable burden or responsibility; esp. in a millstone round one's neck.

10.

The lights are out, the red dress and Jillian gone. You're on the floor. One of the men is behind you breathing in your ear, whispering how your breasts look nice—young with perk. *Nothing ever looks nice in the shadows*, you think, and this is the one truth you will carry, the only certainty to hold onto, as you grow older. In the periphery, Branson's lights will fade along your side.

The man grunts as he pulls the hair at the top of your crown with those hands. He spits the question, *Have you ever?* until your ears and your neck and the side of your left cheek are wet from hot breath. You say *No* when he enters, deep and forceful, the teeth in your jaws rubbing together through the words *please* and *stop*. You aren't conscious of time, but you are aware of the way he pushes back harder as you grab his face, digging nails into rough skin, repeating the words from the bottom of your lungs. His face will go unremembered, only his voice—low and short—when he spoke at you: *Just a little longer*, the voice says. *Good girl.* In the morning, you wake up with blood between your thighs and a missed call from your mother.

11.

Vagina Dentata, /vəˈdʒʌɪnə dɛnˈteɪtə/, [< Latin *dentata*, adj., having teeth, toothed],

> n. (*Cultural Anthropol. and Psychol.*)
>
> > 2. A vagina equipped with teeth occurring in myth, folklore, and religion. Vagina Dentata is a means to silence women, a means to instill fear of women, a means to encourage violence until submission; enslavement

12.

1980 — Jill Riatt *The Journal of the American Academy of Religion*. xlviii. 421. The Taming of Eve: Tertullian, as is now too well known, called woman the gate of hell. He was not speaking as a Christian theologian, although [I'm] sure he thought he was, and so others understood him to have spoken. No, Tertullian was voicing an ancient correlation of woman as "devourer." Female goddesses, driven underground, became hell's gatekeepers from Izangi of Japan to Kore/Persephone.

13.

Queen Elizabeth I, the Virgin Queen, was rumored to suffer from Vagina Dentata. Perhaps she pled with Thomas Seymour to come back after their first shot in the sack. *Let's try one more time*, she might have said, his back to her as he walked away. *Let's try one more time*, she said to herself whenever he was gone. She sat on a bloodied bed, just shy of realizing how alone she would always be.

14.

Hold this whenever you walk by the boys sitting on hallway vents — eyes down, eyes makeup free:

> his low voice, how you cleaned the blood that morning with gas station toilet paper, how, when you finally got home, tears mixed with the warm water of the shower, running down your throat, between your breasts. When you get home, it takes three seconds for your mother to ask about your little

vacation. *It was okay*, you say to her. You tell her, *I just feel dirty*, darting to the bathroom, a locked door.

> Hold it in until you deflate, your throat dry when you will finally tell your secret during a confessional circle at church four months later. One guy will say he smoked weed, another drank too much vodka one night. A girl will admit she's anorexic, but she's trying.

When it's your turn, you will say, *I lost my virginity*. You say, *But I didn't mean to*, face red, eyes looking beyond the edges of the circle. *I lost my virginity, but I didn't mean to*, because you didn't know the right words to communicate, "A man raped me."

15.

Māori legend tells of the gatekeeper of hell—the goddess, Hine-nui-te-pō, who Māui looked to conquer, granting men everlasting life. His father warns him, *Her body is like a woman's, but the pupils of her eyes are greenstone and her hair is kelp. Her mouth is that of a barracuda, and in the place where men enter she has sharp teeth of obsidian.* Māui is crushed by this obsidian, the fate of mankind scarred with mortality. Rather than a woman embodying the sustenance of life, she is instead blamed for mankind's finality.

16.

In Hindu legend, a Rakshasa lived as a tigress, yawning in the grass, scratching her stomach while the cicadas churned. If the spirit happened to catch a man grabbing a woman's shoulders, pressing his body deep and forceful against hers, the tiger would evolve into something sleek, something desirable who could not go untouched: a beautiful woman with curvy edges, mouth corners flicking before seeking retribution. After she seduced the man, the Rakshasa bit back as he entered, treating herself to an erect snack. She fed the rest of the man's body to the other tigers when she was finished.

The Rakshasa went through seven brothers this way. A Hindu god spoke to the eighth brother in a dream. *Get a stick,* the god told the boy. *Shove it inside. Make that Rakshasa, that wicked maneater, bleed like a woman should bleed.*

17.

The church leader will tell your mother, who will sit on the edge of your home's stairs. *Just let me have some space,* you will say, arms limp whenever she hugs your body. Notice how your body will feel like a five-year-old girl's as her fingers brush the crown of your head. Don't swat her hands away.

Later, your brother will come into your room. He will not know what to do with his hands, frantic in the dormant air. You will watch him from your bed. You will tell him, *I'm sorry.*

No. No, no, no, no, he will say, the words staccatoed between sobs and finding his breath. He will walk over to you, putting his arms around you just like your mother did. *I should have been there,* he will tell you. *I should have been there,* saying it again until your comforter is damp with his tears and your pillow is damp from your tears and he can't breathe and you can't breathe, the room folding in on itself.

It's okay, you will tell your brother. *It's okay,* you will tell yourself.

And you will tell yourself the same as a grown woman, grinding your second molars whenever an honest man brushes the nape of your neck, the negative edges of your curves. *You're so beautiful,* the man will say, but his breath will be too hot in your ear, too wet for comfort. So you will think of Elizabeth and the tigress, crossing your arms over whatever you can as you make your body—as you make your*self*—smaller and smaller until he is finished.

Behind the Subway in Chesterfield Village

I backed into the same shitty Ford Taurus twice within the same year in the parking lot behind the Subway in Chesterfield Village. We met there two or three times a week, sitting on the back of Thomas's small maroon pickup, sometimes bringing folding chairs to smoke cigarettes and talk over hardcore music that I pretended to like. On the surface, we were angry teenagers wearing too much makeup with hair in our eyes. I wore black skinny jeans and too-small band T-shirts.

In the summers, we went to a Christian music festival, featuring Tooth and Nail artists, a genre so narrow that we couldn't see outside of ourselves. Someone died swimming in the lake my first year there, and I sat with Thomas, Jon, and Brenna at the edge of the water, watching the search and rescue team taking turns diving to look for the body. By the end of the festival, they still hadn't found it.

Except for me, everyone who met in the parking lot behind the Subway in Chesterfield Village went to a small Christian school on the south side of town. God's Covenant Academy. On Wednesdays, they'd have prayer sessions and Bible studies, and on the weekends, basketball players would swear under their breath when they missed a shot, but the cheerleaders would cheer them on, in short skirts layered over white gym pants to keep them pure of heart. You could tell in a crowd which kids at God's Covenant were my friends—they all wore black in a sea of white and red. Somehow, Brenna and Jon were still nominated for Homecoming court. I still have the handout, featuring the only girl with black eyeliner and the only guy with dark hair swooped across his eyes.

On weekends we didn't attend God's basketball games. Instead, we'd ask our older brothers to buy clove cigarettes, splitting one at a time in between band sets at — oftentimes — Christian venues. Our favorite spot was a coffee shop called NuBrew, doubling as a coffee house during the day and a hip church with kitschy graphic art on Sundays and Wednesdays. I had a crush on the douchebag who promoted almost every show, and sometimes I'd try to make him jealous by standing extra close to Thomas, even though he felt more like a brother. We even shared the same last name. I made the same bad joke the first few times I met him, "Thomas Moore, ha. Did you write *Utopia*?" He didn't laugh, and I'd brush it off, saying there was only one "o" in the More who wrote *Utopia*. Despite these failed attempts at teenage interaction, we became friends.

*

The first time I backed into the shitty Ford Taurus, I laughed it off and sped away, thinking the person likely wouldn't care, that they'd shrug it off like I would have with my own shitty Ford Taurus, the Cli-Taurus. Brenna said, "Oh my God, *Baileyyy*," in a voice that empowered adolescent senselessness rather than some kind of mild reprove, and this only encouraged me to speed away faster.

When I got home, my mom would ask what happened to the back of my car, and I'd shrug: "I don't know. Someone must have backed into me at work."

"Was it anyone we work with?" My first job happened to be at a sandwich shop my mom managed, and she knew every single person on the schedule she made every week. I could see she was checking off the list of employees who would drive that carelessly, but considering the degree of furrowed eyebrows, the math hadn't added up.

I told her no, probably not. "Just bad luck." Her eyebrows went from low to cartoonishly high, and I realized I had said it with a bit of a smile. I told her I had homework and had to prep for a speech tournament in Neosho, which she only believed because I was, in fact, studying whenever I wasn't backing into cars. I had tubs of evidence for policy debate and domestic extemporaneous speaking stacked in the garage to prove it.

*

I was by myself the second time I backed into the shitty Ford Taurus. Sometimes, when everyone else was busy, I'd go to the same spot just to feel less alone and have a reason to not go back home.

Puke Angels

I won't sleep with the guy who made puke angels on the bathroom floor the night of the puke angel incident, but I will the next month when I see him again. By then, Abby will have reminded me on several occasions the way he kept yelling my name from the bathroom, moving his arms up and down in his own vomit, screaming "Baileyyyy" over and over again. She'd reenact the scene for friends in the school courtyard or strangers at our next party. Sometimes, she'd just lean over and whisper, "Hey, Bailey," and I'd say, "Yeah?" and she'd whisper: "pukkkke angelllssss," drawing out the words until it was broken by our laughter.

It will be early May when we have sex in the back seat of his car. He was a year younger than me, but I didn't care because he screamed my name, which meant maybe he thought I was beautiful, even if he yelled it while swimming on top of heaved microwave pizza and stolen vodka from his mother's pantry. He won't yell my name at the back of the car though, and I'll wonder if it was a fluke—him in the puke angel, calling out after me. Then again, I didn't yell out his name in the back of his car, either.

Maybe I was just feeling lonely after breaking it off with my boyfriend at the beginning of the year. It became a two-month stint from late winter that ended with him leaving me a rose attached to a handwritten poem titled "Poem of a Romantic Lover," which terribly upset me because I wasn't a fan of roses or poets, and I especially disliked anyone referring to themselves as a lover, even more so, as it turned out, when it was my own. I ended up writing him my own poem back—"Poem to a Petrarchan Idealist"—which I'll never know if he received, but I won't think about that much whenever I turn in the poem for credit in my English Honors class. The teacher gives me a C because it's a month late, like everything was that semester. In the margins she writes in red ink: *Why is this speaker so angry?*

Dark Center of the Universe

1. Embracing Captain Morgan's Stoicism on an Examination Table

There is a piss-stained corner in the multimedia room, but no one else seems to notice. The children stare at the television screen—Animal Planet, the go-to channel for a youth psychiatric ward, apparently. An orca calf swims along its mother on the screen. It feels happy and free, I hope. The children's faces look removed altogether. A boy sits in the closet. He is seven, maybe eight. Eleven? *I don't know. Children all look the same age*, I think. The boy looks down at his hands, dissecting them unyieldingly for three hours. I arrived here after my mother picked me up from work, placing me between my youth pastor and a family friend. She said we had to go. That I shouldn't worry. *She just didn't know what to do with me anymore.*

She said this again when she left the front desk four hours ago, right before one of the nurses guided me into a small room just down hall. Everything was painted white, blaring. The nurse sat in a swivel chair, rolling the wheels along with each absent nod of her head as she looked down at my paperwork. The room grew brighter and smelled more medical, more unfeeling, with every mindless click of her pen.

The nurse explained how we were just going to go over a few questions and then give me a basic physical. Her voice remained mechanical. I nodded absently, only taking in a breath of stale hospital air, my heart beating too fast to stay in sync with the room's lone decoration: a standard white-faced clock, its ticks the only source of noise besides the off-beat click of her pen. Hollowed time echoed off the white walls, the white paper lining the examination table. It even echoed off the white teeth of the nurse in front of me, a woman who shook her clean-cut bangs out of her eyes while she twisted her brunette hair, as if bored.

She smiled with all her teeth. Her name tag read STEPHANIE. Of course her name was Stephanie, matching her humble engagement ring, her ironed lavender scrubs, and French manicured nails. I would have thought this regardless of whatever her name was, if I had the courage to be honest with myself.

"Okay," Stephanie said, "let's start. Don't be scared. These are just basic questions. You'll talk to a psychiatrist tomorrow over deeper matters."

Did I look scared? Angry, surely—but scared? Or was that a go-to platitude for new patients regardless of why they were there to begin with? Did I look more like a ghost than usual, my pale complexion even more washed out by unbearably white walls? Were the clock's ticks making me appear even more unhinged, eyeballs rolling into the back of my skull out of irritation, confusion, exhaustion—an angsty Captain Hook with uneven bangs and day-old makeup? I had so many questions for Stephanie, but she already prefaced our relationship with the inability to answer the deeper questions.

Not knowing what to do, I told her okay and mirrored her tooth-drenched smile with too much enthusiasm.

"How often do you drink?"

I tell her once or twice a month.

I think: *As much as I can get. I wish I had a drink right now! These walls are too fucking white, and I'm a bored seventeen-year-old who's convinced she has* ADD *complemented with back-burner depression and perpetual anxiety. I have a hovering mother, a mother who found her second love in Jesus Christ himself when she joined a Southern Baptist church after my father left her.*

How much do you drink when you do?

The truth: *I don't know. Whatever is there and all at once, until I'm smiling freely, until I forget. Until I'm not myself and my new self is someone more charming to others—not others like you or my mom, Stephanie, but others who read* Franny and Zooey *and say shit like* Kafkaesque *even though*

Kafkaesque may be the most bullshit thing anyone has ever said in my entire existence and perhaps even the history of the world, before Kafka was even born, human or cockroach.

What I said: "Just a few, enough to get a warm buzz."

She paused with this answer, and the clock stilled with her.

She told me we were doing this so she could help me. How, in my mom's statement, she wrote that she brought me here because she thought I was going to hurt myself, how she woke up this morning to me crawling through the window. How she took me to work because I smelled like alcohol.

"Please be honest with me," Stephanie said.

"Yes, sure," I said. "Of course."

"Glad we're on the same page," she said. "And when's the last time you drank?"

"Last night."

"How much did you drink?"

A fifth of Captain Morgan. There's even a picture of me standing like the Captain with my foot on a chair, face STOIC AS HELL *as my eyes looked past the lens.*

"Just a few drinks."

She sighed, writing a note on the pad of paper. "Drug use?"

"No, just the occasional drink," I said, knowing last night's weed would show up on the urine test. In the back of my mind, I vaguely remember someone bringing opium, which was such a weird thing for anyone to bring, but what did I know? I had only ever drank and smoked pot. One time I bought Adderall, but that only quieted my addled brain, so it didn't feel like I could count that as much of anything at all.

I go over Stephanie's questions whenever I walked away from the medical room and into the worn multimedia room. The boy in the closet looks up from his hands. We make eye contact, our faces blank, unmoving. Was it a boy like him who left the carpet uncleaned, the staff too busy with paperwork to recognize the smell of urine? For a moment my brain wonders if it had been a seventeen-year-old girl who was just like me. I wonder if she would have also resented a nurse like Stephanie, not because of her invasive questions but because of her normalcy, her unstained lavender scrubs that scream contentment in a way I thought I would never understand.

2. Teenage Girl as Dark Center of the Universe

Copernicus was a buzzkill to geocentrists, the Catholic church, and sad teenagers, and despite being only one of the three, you maintain seventeen-year-old self-importance without hesitation. During a college astronomy course, you will find yourself identifying with Harlow Shapley, who, in 1918, discovered how our own solar system wasn't the center of the Milky Way galaxy. We're not even a quarter of the way in, the professor will tell you, who, like the rest of the class, is struggling through a rough emergence of cosmological loneliness. Shapley was also from southwest Missouri—a fact you can't shake—and you'll wonder if his fascination with the cosmos stemmed from wanting to find something bigger than your home. Something bigger than yourself. He died in Boulder, Colorado, just twenty minutes from where you were born. You hope this isn't a bad omen for your own life, this swapping of place.

"So, what is the center?" you will ask. It's 2013, and you're certain there is an answer to everything. But you're a philosophy major, and Wittgenstein's Tractatus Seven always rings in the back of your mind: Whereof we cannot speak, we must pass over in silence.

"A supermassive black hole," the astronomy professor responds with a too-generous smile. For the most part, you enjoy this ancient man, how he seems all-knowing about astronomy even though he admits with humility that he, in fact, knows very little. You like his jokes about the density of Saturn, how, if you had a big enough bathtub, the planet would float (but it'd leave you behind rings when it was finished!). The professor's answer brings you back to every country drive you've taken the past nine years, times when you listened to Modest Mouse's album *The Moon and Antarctica* until you realized you were low on gas and had three dollars left in your bank account. Until you realized, at some point, you always had to go back home.

Even after the astronomy course ends that summer, you will still find yourself on those same roads as you sing the lyrics: "I'm not the dark center of the universe like you thought." As a teenage girl who was often told that there was something dark about her, something angry or something that needed to be fixed, you disagreed with the song, the rhythm of the drum matching the heartbeat in your throat. But you sang anyway, the road knowing your voice more than any other thing or any other person in the universe.

3. Kansas City Gangs and Apathetic Tae Bo

The nurse won't let me take my prescribed dosage of Prozac until all the lab results are back. This is the third time someone has said "waiting for the lab results," which causes me to worry, only assuming the worst: perhaps I had cancer; perhaps I contracted HIV from the two people I had slept with; perhaps I'm already dead. *Surely the latter*, I think.

It is the second day of my psychiatric stay, a term I have trouble saying out loud in front of workers or even the other patients, most of whom are under thirteen, nonverbal, and generally dejected. I didn't sleep the night before—I couldn't get my mind to rest, especially after hearing the first mention of awaited lab results. Also because of Brandy.

During Animal Planet, Brandy caused an "episode," as the staff called it, while talking to someone over the phone. Screaming at the person on the other end, Brandy threw the phone across the hallway, barely missing the two children on the couch. Three of the staff grabbed her and took her into the examination room I had been in only hours before. Through the crack in the door, I could see two of the staff holding her down while the other tried to put on restraints. She quieted after minutes of yelling. Perhaps they sedated her, like a wild dog. After, I learned she was my roommate, but she ended up sleeping somewhere else the first night, and she didn't say where when we sat at the table for breakfast the next morning.

Without us asking, she tells us what happened.

"I was angry because I was trying to explain to my mom that they wouldn't give me my medicine," she says. She adds that she needs to have her medicine.

"Sorry," I tell her, which I mean, but I'm more concerned with the fact that I wasn't being given my medicine either. I had been distant but tame since my arrival. I didn't know what put me in the same category as Brandy, except for the mere existence of being here at all.

She asks why I'm here, a bit of egg falling out of her mouth.

I tell her I'm not really sure.

And I still really wasn't sure, especially after her previous night's episode or my being relatively sitting-in-closet-free. And I really, really wasn't sure when, before taking a swig of her milk, she told me how, when she got out of the hospital, she was going to steal her foster mom's car, drive to Kansas City, and join a gang.

"My dad lives there," I say—a failed attempt at connection. "Are there actually gangs in Kansas City?"

Brandy laughs too loudly, and I look down at my milk carton, wondering if I should be embarrassed.

After breakfast, morning exercise is scheduled. A staff member puts in a DVD, and everyone—patients and staff alike—watch in unison as Billy Blanks materializes on the screen, preaching how "a will is to make a decision how you should take care of yourself!"

I feel my face grow red during the warm up, wondering if anyone noticed how goofy it all was: Billy Blanks in an orange tank top, demanding determination, demanding will, from a group of mentally exhausted children from ages five to seventeen while a handful of adults watched, arms crossed and indifferent.

4. Blood Sisters Venture to Watch Blood Brothers Away from Home

In musty music venues, you'd smoke Camels with Abby, your faces dimly lit by hanging stained-glass lamps. It was 2005, and your closet consisted of band T-shirts, paisley handkerchiefs, and jeans that clung to hips that shouldn't belong to a teenager—curves that often made you blush when they finally brought the kind of attention you tried so hard for. You always felt bulky and looming next to Abby, a girl two years younger who weighed less than a hundred pounds and was a dozen jean sizes smaller than you. You'd try to justify the weight difference by telling yourself that you're tall for a girl, how some women would love to be five eight. Some women might even want your curves along with it. But despite physical appearance, you both carried yourselves similarly: sassy and unapologetic, biting humor with a weakness for unreachable, dogshit guys. You also had closeted eating disorders and felt trapped in your bodies.

Abby and you went to bars to watch bands every week, hiding the M's on your minor-aged hands to steal drinks from older friends when no one was watching. It became easier to convince your mom to go with the freedom your beloved gray '95 Ford Taurus—*the Cli-Taurus*—offered, as well as your ability to manipulate the plans. Like in May 2005, one month before you find yourself in a psychiatric unit. You told your mother you wanted to visit your father in Kansas City, less than a three-hour drive from your home in Springfield. You painted a picture of the sky and the ground, an epistolary note left in the middle of the picture saying how you needed a break for a moment—you needed to get out of Springfield and out of your own head. "Don't worry about me," you told her. "I'll be okay," you said. A woman named Stephanie will tell you your mother thought this was a suicide note, which will make you cry in a lone hospital bed because you worry that you don't even know how to communicate to her through writing, the only medium you feel like you can untangle yourself.

But you weren't planning on seeing your dad. The Blood Brothers, a band you acted like you knew, were playing in Lawrence, Kansas. You were going to stop by on the way to say hi to your dad, so mostly you weren't lying. Fueled with snorted coffee, you spent the night collecting change and selling gift cards to strangers. You made fifty bucks, enough for cigarettes and gas to make the trip.

The Cli-Taurus didn't have AC and the CD player broke the week before, so you couldn't play *The Moon and Antarctica*. Instead, you were forced to listen to radio stations. You'll call in asking the DJ for a request to stop playing Green Day's "Boulevard of Broken Dreams." He'll laugh. "Sorry, it's still on the top hits," he'll explain, but you ignore him, saying that hearing it for the four hundredth time that day is making you feel murderous. It was particularly hot for June, which adds a bit of mania to your laughter as you hung up the phone.

You chain-smoked cigarettes, asking Abby to light one up every time because, even though no one else knows except for your mother, you've never driven on a highway for this long. And this will especially make you nervous when the two-laned Highway 13 turns into a four-lane interstate between KC and Lawrence. It would have made you nervous to know Kansas City had gangs, but you would be unaware of this fact until next month.

Thirty minutes away from the venue, heavy rain muddled your line of vision, and you asked Abby to light your cigarettes with more urgency. You finally arrive, more alive from the adrenaline.

5. Psychiatrist as Dark Center of the Universe

Modest Mouse tells us how if we go straight long enough in the universe, we'll end up right back where we started. When I get the chance to talk to the psychiatrist the afternoon of my second day at the hospital, I was perplexed to find my limitless backroad driving and perpetual avoidance issues had led me back to being the same person, in the same situation, but with more problems. Perhaps it was the fact that, despite moving constantly in my car—music too loud as an attempt to mute my muddled head—I really wasn't moving anywhere at all, the car's motion only offering emotional immobility. Another Zeno's Paradox.

The psychiatrist keeps talking at me, talking down to me. I wish I could mute him out with ambient noise.

"What do you think you're going to do?" he asks. He just told me I was pregnant, every word still hanging in the air, mixing together.

But there isn't a clock in his office, and the lack of echoed ticks creates an uneasy silence in the room. I don't know how long I sat there looking at him before I could answer: "I don't know."

"Do you know who the father is?" he asks.

It could be one of two people, but I remain quiet, staring straight ahead, past him like I stared past the camera lens as Captain Morgan two nights ago. I found myself more perplexed that had happened two nights ago than hearing a sterile psychiatrist tell me my urine sample came back positive for pregnancy, how every staff member had known but treated me as if I were a child who didn't deserve to hear the results.

I think back to my physical with Stephanie and a forgotten question resurfaces: *When was your last period?*

I didn't know—I couldn't remember. Monitoring menstrual cycles was something I didn't think much about in between debate tournaments, LiveJournal posts, and smiling shyly at boys during concerts. Menstrual cycles were another back-burner category, another checkmark on my avoidance list.

There was no way Stephanie could have known at that point. She hadn't yet administered the cup for my urine sample. Even still, after the positive test came back, staff members could have shouted the word *pregnancy* at me, and I still wouldn't have known. *We can't give you your medicine until your pregnancy test comes back*, one would hint. *Do you normally weigh this much?* a younger male asked. He was only trying to figure out how far along I was, but in my female mind, the question only caused me to grow more insecure about my wide hips.

How could anyone expect me to be able to handle raising a child? I couldn't even tell how old the closet boy was. I couldn't even regulate my own menstrual clock. The worst part about it was I had a sneaking suspicion, but it only surfaced once when I questioned whether pregnancy was a possibility. It was a month ago, alone in a hotel room, stolen vodka on the windowsill.

The psychiatrist interrupted my internal ramblings, saying, "Usually we want you to stay forty-eight hours before having someone visit, but I think this circumstance warrants your mother visiting."

He hands me a telephone. "Give her a call," he says.

And all I managed to comprehend was the word "mother" falling from his mouth too loudly for the comfort the etymology presupposed.

6. Stolen Vodka for the Heart, Soul, and Uterus

You pour vodka stolen from a hometown grocery store in two Styrofoam hotel cups, one for you and one for Abby. Your father paid for the hotel with points, unaware the lengths you had lied to come to a concert you felt quarter-hearted about while searching for a boy you had a crush on while the band played the songs you pretended to know. He said he was going to be there, but he never showed up, a fact you dwelled on throughout the night, even when Abby talked fast, excited about the opening band, how she got "sensual chills" over the way the lead singer moved against the microphone stand, how he may as well have tongued the microphone. It was all so alarmingly erotic.

And it was erotic, even for you, lost in the melancholy abyss of Petrarchan high school ideology. Abby and you weren't all that experienced when it came to sexual relationships. Naturally a metal pole and a man's narrowed hips mixed with dissonant screeches yelled blatant eroticism.

Back at the hotel, you both take the Styrofoam cups outside, sipping the vodka without anything mixed, without anything to chase it with. You liked getting drunk fast, so you devour liquor straight and in gulps, each drink making your shoulders looser, the worries you had already pushed aside, growing fainter: grades, money, mother, a breakup, the last time you had your period. It's the last item on the checklist that you couldn't forget entirely, even as you faded on top of starchy hotel sheets. Abby was out smoking or perhaps she was flirting with the front desk clerk who, despite his pink triangle tattoo and boyfriend references, you both tried to convince wasn't gay and that, instead, he should make out with one of you. Or both of you, everyone all at once.

But when he finally said, "You girls need to go to bed," you listened, despite your mother's words echoing in your head: *That girl was stubborn, even in the womb.* It's the word *womb* repeating over and over in your brain that brought a need to be alone. You told Abby you were going to go upstairs. You'd be right back, you said, aware she still had an unlit cigarette to start and finish.

Between your sight doubling and the rate of your heart picking up from all the things you've left buried, the hallway to your hotel room felt limitless. Like the fact you never went to class anymore, no longer caring about getting above a 4.0 GPA. You had taken honors classes all throughout high school, prioritized debate tournaments and extracurriculars until last semester when you met Abby, another bored girl looking for distractions.

Your mother, who, after your brother moved out for college, had targeted all her excess worry towards you—an opportune time considering your increasing lack of care. There was a breakup in March when you turned seventeen. "Poor guy," your mother would say when you told her the news. "He was so good for you," which really meant he went to church with us and played guitar for the youth group. And then, at the bottom of it all, was the fact you lost track of when you last had your period, dismissing pregnancy because you had spotted blood a few months ago. Nothing to worry about it.

When you finally reached the hotel room, you collapsed on top of the comforter. As the air conditioner hissed, you found your knuckles meeting your stomach, as if the pressure could make everything go away. *If anything was there at all*, you convinced yourself before falling asleep, lights on, world dark.

7. A Discrepancy in the Color of Cars

Brandy chose the red car, and she does so with pizzazz. She finally got her medication, she told me before group game time. Which means Brandy wasn't pregnant—*probably just crazy*, I think with a hint of spite. The thought doesn't give me a new sense of fortification. Everything is blank, neither on the defensive nor working toward making an effort, a decision.

The only other patient there is Wayne since the younger children are in the gym for their own group session. Wayne was thirteen with long dirty-blond hair. Both him and Brandy wore their clothes loose around their bodies. Both him and Brandy carried their sadness with an edge to them, in a way I had never seen, never looking anyone directly in the eye and staring at the table when asked a question.

The activity for the teenagers was a knock-off version of the board game LIFE, featuring questions and consideration for self-improvement. It was only four o'clock on the second day, and all I could think about was my mother coming during visiting hours.

"Pick your favorite color," one of the staff members says.

Brandy grabs red. Wayne reaches for the green car, placing it on the large section marked "BEGINNINGS." I grab the closest car to me—a blaring white. A lack of color, like the walls lining every room and hall in this section of the hospital, like Stephanie's teeth and monotony.

Brandy goes first, flicking the arrow which would lead her bull of a car to "WELL-BEING." She's encouraged to pick up the corresponding card. She refuses. "I don't want to," she says. "You can't make me."

The staff say maybe next time.

Wayne spins the arrow, and it lands on "FAMILY." He picks up the card after moving forward two spaces.

"What can you do to better relationships with your family?" He reads the card out loud, everyone waiting.

Wayne is quiet, staring out past the card.

"Wayne, what can you do?" one of the staff members asks, repeating the question as if Wayne had misunderstood, as if he was slow.

The answer comes out of his mouth, and for a moment, it snaps me out of the whiteness of my thoughts: He doesn't know how to improve relationships with his family. His father is in jail for theft. His grandfather is in prison for raping Wayne when he was a child. And he's here, in this place, because his mother found him nearly dead after taking a cocktail of pills from the bathroom cabinet.

Instead of a blinding numbness, I am wild with discomfort. I look at the staff to see what guidance they offered, but they remain nonplussed, empty.

"Good," one staff member finally tells him. But the response coupled with everything in the moment felt arbitrary. Wayne cries, and I want to do something for him, but I don't know how to comfort a crying child.

One of the staff shifts the focus back to me. "White car, go," he says.

I suddenly feel overwhelmed in the whiteness of the place, the whiteness of the plastic car. I wanted to be back in my own car — my real car — driving on backroads and drowning out all the noise. My grubby Taurus, its shade somewhere in between the structure of white walls and the dark center of the universe.

I look at the arrow, offering all kinds of life directions to take. But I don't know how to tell them I wasn't sure how to go forward or if I could even go back, and, more importantly, that I didn't know the difference between the two.

The End of the Rainbow

June

When it got too quiet, we opted for music, listening to the soundtrack to *A Mighty Wind* because it was the only music we could agree on. Perhaps because it was the one CD that wasn't contemporary Christian music in my mother's car. Or maybe we listened to the album over & over again because I couldn't stand the idea of the unbroken silence stilling between us, only to be interrupted by "How are you feeling?" or "What are you thinking?" or the most pressing question that lay underneath it all: "What are you going to do?"

 Catherine O' Hara and Eugene Levy were the only voices that could bring me comfort in between gun show signs and anti-abortion billboards.

 Ever since I had been an awkward fifteen-year-old trying to grow into herself, I had loved Christopher Guest films, and there was a certain joy and nurturing that came with the music of his third mockumentary, especially when my favorite duo's voices—*Mitch and Mickey*—merged into a slow ballad, a yearning of missed love I romanticized since my first viewing.

*

We've always opted for country drives when the world felt too heavy, even when we could hardly afford the gas. In June 2005, unleaded is $1.71 a gallon, which means five dollars is enough to go the long way to Branson. I always avoided heading south any time I drove alone, but it's hard to tell your mother not to go somewhere because someone hurt you there when you were fourteen. The air in the car is heavy enough with the news that I was now stupid pregnant. She didn't pick up on the apprehension whenever it took me too long to say, "Okay, sounds good," but maybe anywhere felt better than the too-white hospital with sad children and that insufferable woman at the front desk. That and I couldn't avoid disappointing my mother any more than I already had.

Our windows were both down—the early summer heat just high enough to warm our skin without the heavy-handedness of humidity that comes with July and August. We listened to the soundtrack to *A Mighty Wind* on repeat, and I would ask her again and again if we could replay "Kiss at the End of the Rainbow."

When I was a child, my mother would sing lullabies on nights sleep didn't come easy, which was most nights. Her final song was never enough, and I'd always ask for more. Even when I couldn't think of another song, I'd ask for the same one again. My favorite song was "Hush Little Baby," and I'd have her sing it over and over again. Falling asleep, I would think of all the gifts the mother would buy for her baby. A diamond ring is such a stupid thing for a child to have, and a mockingbird always felt rude. Unlike the child in "Hush Little Baby," I just wanted one more song, even if it was nonsense. I could never get enough time with her, just like how on the drive to Branson, I couldn't get enough of Catherine O'Hara and Eugene Levy.

I'll realize nearly fifteen years later that "Kiss at the End of the Rainbow" was a description of a suspension between worlds. One world—an enchanting space colored with fairy tales and dreams—represented a childhood I needed to cling onto, regardless of how much I tried to push away girlhood and innocence. And that other world is one I had always hoped for, despite it feeling fleeting and undeserved: a forever and secure love that was *more precious than a pot of gold*.

*

Passengers can see the historical trajectory of anti-abortion rhetoric from Missouri billboards lining interstate highways. The sanctity-of-life-driven advertisements become more and more sparse the farther you travel away from the Ozarks, so you can imagine how overbearing their presence is on a state highway from Springfield, Missouri, to

Branson. I restrained audible sighs with each amassing pro-life sign, all showcasing fat, happy, white babies with wide smiles. *Our hearts beat 18 days after conception! I had eyes 14 days after conception! A Nation that Kills Children is a Nation without Hope.* LET YOUR BABY LIVE!!!

July

Everyone was asking what I was going to do. I mostly answered the same: I don't know. Maybe that's why I won't remember particular instances of sharing the news—they all sort of melded into each other, creating a white noise I'll do my best to avoid. Except for Thomas, the only friend who shared the same last name as me. He said, "Looks like I'm going to be an uncle!" I told him over the phone, but I could hear him smiling big on the other end.

By July, I eventually did tell everyone in my life who mattered enough. On the Fourth, a group of friends were getting together to celebrate AMERICA! at some campgrounds in Branson. My mother agreed to let me go, said it would be good for me to get out, so I found myself in Branson again for the second time in a month. I'll never tell anyone how, both times, we drove past the hotel I tried so hard to avoid.

We took turns lying in the bed of Thomas's pickup truck. I will still look for this pickup when I drive by his childhood home, even years later as an adult, despite knowing it isn't there. His parents junked it whenever Thomas ran into a tree off the side of the highway at one in the morning. In two years and some change from now, he will rest in a coffin with eighth notes and quarter notes sprinkled around the rim. My mother will come to his reception, catch me sitting with Abby and Brenna in the pews. I won't cry until she hugs me, and I don't even try to hold in the sob or conceal the leftover alcohol on my breath. I won't realize how much I needed her until she was there.

For now, Thomas is here, and we are spending this time by making animals out of the spaces between tree leaves. I had just found a sad owl when Thomas realized he was out of cigarettes and needed to go into town to get more. I was the only who could drive.

Outside of the campsite, the world had turned green. Storm clouds rolled in from the west, creating a stark contrast to what light was left right before dusk. At any given moment, the clouds could have broken with a heavy pour, and Thomas kept asking, "Do you think we'll make it back in time?"

I felt like the wrong person to answer any question regarding time, but I told him I think we may get lucky. On our way back, we passed a pro-life billboard, but the light was faltering, its flickers adding to the flashes of lightning in the background.

*

My mother and I were both nervous with sweat, and the rising summer heat demanded continuous AC. Our windows were rolled up on the drive between our house and the Pregnancy Care Center. No music, only nervous, terse sentences during the twenty-minute trip. I had asked her to take the long way there.

When we arrived, another lady at another front desk asked me to fill out the required forms and answer the required questions. *I don't know how far along I am. I don't know what I want to do with the baby. I don't know how I feel about adoption. Yes, abortion is an option. I am seventeen years old.*

I had been warned by a friend whose mother volunteered at the PCC that if you mark abortion as a potential choice, the women who worked there would try to talk you out of it. When I was handed the papers, I looked at the boxes of options I had:

> ☐ Keep Baby
> ☐ Put Baby up for Adoption
> ☐ Abort Baby

All three possibilities contained the word I kept ignoring. *Baby* may as well have been in all caps, in bold, italicized, underlined, and in bloodred. I checked all three and returned it to the woman at the front desk, watching her look at the paper and slowly nod, making a few notes I couldn't see. She looked back at me with a frown, said it would be a few minutes.

In the ultrasound room, another woman asked me to raise my shirt and told me to prepare myself for something cold. My body lay flat on an already cold examination table. I wondered how many girls in my same position had been on the same bed, folding their arms out of the discomfort of seldomly sharing their body with another human, whether for medicinal purposes or sexual. She slathered a sticky jelly across my stomach, just cool enough it made every muscle tense more than they already were. The moment the gel hit my skin, I felt outside of my own body, alien to myself. I closed my eyes, thinking maybe this was just a deep dream I couldn't climb out of.

I felt my mother grab my hand, and suddenly I was crying. I couldn't remember the last time we had touched each other out of love, the last time she had held me to nurture rather than to hold back my welling teenage hormones. I opened my eyes and looked down at our hands. Even though they were nearly the same size, my hands looked so small in her own.

The nurse interrupted the moment with the announcement that she had found a beating heart, causing both my mother's and my chests to fall from a held breath we hadn't known we had been holding.

"Look at that," the nurse said. "A true miracle!" And though I was annoyed at the loaded religious subtext, prepared that she was about to talk me out of one of my three options, I couldn't help but do a double take of the pulsing mass on the screen. "Now wouldn't it be a shame to let that gift of life go?"

I didn't answer, and even if I had known how to respond, I probably wouldn't have, especially when her next comment changed everything: "Looks like you're already four and a half months along."

I did the math quicker than my mom, and I saw the moment she realized the time I had to make a decision had drastically reduced to just a few weeks. Six weeks until my third trimester, the cutoff for legal abortion in Missouri in 2005. Sixteen years later, the Supreme Court would overturn *Roe*, and Missouri would be the first one in line—just minutes after the announcement—to make abortion illegal after six weeks of pregnancy.

My mother's eyes flashed when she caught up. My heart pumped outside of my chest, and I didn't know if I should worry whether the hurried beats would affect what was in the pit of my belly.

*

I'll adapt to calling the baby a baby rather than my initial preferred designation: *it*. I still won't have a name because I won't be gifted a baby name book until August. *The Best Baby Name Book in the Whole Wide World*, a present from a church shower the congregation held only a handful of weeks after the pastor read my letter of apologies and shame—my *testimony*—during a late July sermon. I wasn't there for my own testimony. I couldn't stand to hear those words spoken by a pastor who, days prior, had edited my version to look like a call for forgiveness, a lesson of obedience and chastity. I remember a friend telling me afterward how the pastor said he wished I could have been in attendance that day, but I wasn't lying when I wrote how I was worried they would no longer accept me, how I didn't know how to come back to this home.

August

In August, the Ozarks air is heavy with humidity. Between the failing AC and my growing belly, I felt unhinged.

The Pregnancy Care Center released its monthly newsletter, highlighting a teenage girl who had been on the verge of aborting an unborn angel until the heroes of the PCC saved another life with their powers of persuasion gifted by God himself. The newsletter glorified its efforts under its self-given acronym, which prompted me to purposely switch the conservative nonprofit with other abbreviations representing much different ideologies: "PCP saved my life, my fucking Being this summer," "ICP has a hot write-up about teenage sex, featuring meeeeeeee." I knew nothing about the drug PCP, and I knew nothing about Insane Clown Posse except they liked Faygo soda, didn't know how magnets worked, and they had a logo that looked eerily similar to the soldier on the cover of Joseph Heller's *Catch-22*, which was what the narrative of my life was beginning to feel like.

For a second time, my mother sat with me in an ultrasound room, except on this occasion it was in a hospital that was free from political bias, or more inconspicuous about it anyway. The nurse said, "This may be cold" only seconds before spreading the jelly across my stomach. The cold goo still made me feel like an alien, as if I was outside of myself. When it first touched my stomach, I thought of a Teenage Mutant Ninja Turtle toy my brother had played with a decade before, a torture device called the "Flushomatic," which poured ooze onto a turtle in order to reveal his secrets.

Weeks later, we still don't have a name, but we know he's a boy. I'll tell this to the first person who asks, and I'll tell it again to the hundredth person. I always used a first-person communal when I talked because it made me feel less alone. It was the last month of my second trimester, I had only lived the reality of being pregnant for eight weeks, and I still didn't know if any of my choices would be the right one for me. In my corner of Missouri, most of the people in my life—regardless of how small their presence was within it—had a hot take on my best course of action, and it was always an opinion that left my bodily autonomy out of question. Even in someone's silence, I could feel the weight of their opinion. I could read it in their eyes, the way they cocked their head and looked beyond my body, beyond me. Especially my mother's. Every morning, I woke up feeling like a teenage mutant who made people feel uncomfortable, but I didn't have a Splinter I could trust for objective guidance, and that's the only thing I really needed: a wise rat to tell me what to do.

Choices

2005

The girl didn't know how to tell her brother about the pregnancy, but it spilled out of the corners of her mouth in one way or another.

Her brother said *okay* and breathed, and the girl said *okay* and forgot to breathe.

He said *this is going to be tough*, and she may have cried at that point. He reworded it:

Well, he said to the girl, there are three things we can do. You can keep the child, which will be hard. You can put it up for adoption, which will also be hard. Or you can have an abortion, and that would be hard, too.

She won't remember her response, just the relief that came with someone not pressuring her in one direction or another.

2022

The pregnant girl who sat on the couch talking about choices with her brother is now a woman, though she will always feel just shy of adulthood. When she looks back to that moment on the couch, the image of the girl remains the same—eyes down, mouth tight. She's pale and glowing and lost. An apparition caught in memory.

Every time the woman remembers the ghosts she carries, a burning desperation spreads throughout her body. All she wants to do is hold the girl, tell her everything will be all right. *You're braver than you think.*

She will also think about Heidegger.

The memory of a Continental philosophy class plays out, almost too vivid: a mousy professor welcomes class as he writes on the chalkboard.

When he's finished, a question in all caps asks: WHY ARE THERE BEINGS INSTEAD OF NOTHINGS?

He's smiling, which happens so infrequently that it felt more unnerving than friendly. He waits for the last student to shuffle in before announcing that we had finally done it—we made it to the ontology unit.

He scrawls *choices* and *non-choices* underneath his original question, circling the words over and over again. Next, the professor turns around and adjusts his round wire frames before saying, "Heidegger says we are the choices we make, and the choices we do not make." He does a quick scan of the class. His glasses slip down his nose again. "This is important because it means the choices you make define you and show what kind of life you want to lead. Choices qualify Being."

The professor pauses, allowing time to process. He pushes up his glasses again, waiting for the slower notetakers to finish writing. "It sounds pretty neat until you realize this means endless possibilities . . . and that leads to . . ." He turns to the board again and writes ANXIETY!!!

*

The girl won't yet understand why it bothers her when the professor says, "Embracing the freedom of choice allows you to lead a life of authenticity." But as a woman, she'll get caught up on the word *choice*, remembering that girl on the other side of the couch who felt like she didn't have an infinity of possibilities. Just a list of three. And even then, she remembered how people not-so-subtly tried to sway her away from the last option on the list, how the layering of voices was so loud that it made her feel like it could never be a choice or even a non-choice at all, as if it was simply a word left unspoken.

Step Two

How to Hold a Baby

First, open your arms wide, as if you were accepting something you always wanted. Remember the first time you held a baby? You were at a party, nearly eight years old, and a mother you hardly knew and your own mother hardly knew, had trusted you to hold fifteen pounds of something sacred. The time of year was spring, and it was warm enough now to wear shorts and let the sun hit your skin. When the being rests in your arms, it will look like layers of baby fat holding one another up. *This is something beautiful*, you'll think, which is such a serious thing for a child to say to herself. At that point, you knew you'd always want to be a mother, to hold your own child. *A girl*, hopefully, you told the adults watching you carefully, and they'd laugh in glee. *How cute. How Sweet. How innocent.* This taught you the second rule about holding: look like you know what you're doing.

As an adult, you'll project insecurities onto this first memory, and it obfuscates reality. Did you really, one minute in, have a flash of anxiety you were going to drop the baby on its head? In your fabricated memory, anxiety takes shape like a watermelon bursting on the ground.

As an adult, you'll remember this moment was shortly before your idea of family was shattered. How long after your own father left did you decide you'd never want to be a mother, that you could never have your heart broken into millions of pieces like the woman looking out the window as she pets the family dog, crying just low enough she thinks no one can hear her?

Piece by Piece

Life fell into a rhythm of puzzles and watching late night *X-Files* reruns when sleep didn't come easy, which it never did. No matter how far ahead we move in time or who she is talking to, my mother says the same thing: "She was so much nicer then."

I'd feign a weak smile, looking down, never mentioning how the same thing could have been said about her.

Maybe if we had never stopped doing puzzles, I'd still be a nicer person. At the very least, we'd experience the calmness that came with filling in negative space with the confidence that we possessed all the necessary pieces needed to make something whole. If we could figure out its edges, the rest would fall into place, piece by piece.

There was even a reference image on the front of the box when we needed a reminder of the bigger picture, the end we were both working toward.

At the table, we'd sometimes listen to the radio, singing along to Garth Brooks or Reba McEntire. In other moments, I'd place a scratched CD containing Beethoven sonatas in my Discman and press the headphones against my growing stomach. Maybe *Moonlight Sonata* or *Für Elise*—something to fall asleep to, to be calmed by so he could also benefit from the stillness of puzzles.

When I finished a section, I'd read a few paragraphs from *What to Expect When You're Expecting* or circle baby names from *The Best Baby Name Book in the Whole Wide World*. When I was unsure about a name, I'd test it out on my mother, whose facial expressions always betrayed her if she wasn't into something. The names I loved were added to a handwritten list at the back of the book, but I found myself circling back to the same two. One name was a result of being a teenager rife with unchecked emotions and fresh off her first read of *Catcher in the Rye*. The other name because my stolen copy of *Guero* played on repeat any time I found myself unraveling from the bigger picture lingering just beyond next week's puzzle.

At the other end of the table my mother would be on a hunt for a particular piece, dragging the box while in search of a shared color scheme or a connecting pattern. If a puzzle's complexity required it, she'd take her organization to another level, deconstructing each silhouette by the placement of its respective interjambs and blanks. This strategy manifested in haphazard piles wherever free table space permitted, each mound containing pieces sharing its structural form. To someone else, it might look like a chaotic assemblage of nonsense. To us, it was a codified system that helped us navigate something difficult.

Other times, we'd work on the puzzles in silence, the quiet only interrupted when we'd exchange commentary on our progression: "Oh, I finished the road." "Oh, I finished the mother whale." "Oh, I found the last edge piece." Finding the last edge piece always offered more relief than expected because it meant we hadn't lost something that we had already chalked up as missing.

Another recurring discussion was the shape of puzzle pieces, which aren't universal. They vary in interjamb and blank placement. They vary widely in thickness and size. "Like penises," my mom would point out as a response to her own observation.

Her humor had always been dirty—despite the kind of church she went to. When a pastor said something hinting toward innuendo, I could feel her suck in a held breath, the pew shaking from withheld laughter. On more than one occasion, she baked a penis cake, and her dreams were often plagued with having a nine-foot dick, which, as she always said, made it hard to go around corners. Then she'd laugh at the word "hard," and I'd laugh, too.

Puzzles created a comfortable space — moments where reality didn't feel so weighed down, and I didn't feel at the center of chaos. In that moment, we were just a mother and daughter doing something we loved, laughing at varying sizes and shapes of puzzles and penises, and trying to learn to love each other again.

I'll learn later that a woman dreaming of possessing a penis may be some Freudian foil to her waking life: "You are affirming power or dominance," I'll read in an interpretative dream guide in a musty corner of a used bookstore. Power has always felt like a slippery slope to me, which is interesting because a slippery slope is also a logical fallacy.

My mother was strict in the sense that she was unwavering in her decisions and rules because it was the only way she felt some sense of control over two unruly teenagers. But by the time I was sixteen, my brother had moved out. In his absence, she focused that leftover energy on me. It created a wedge, which I would hold on to harder than I needed to. It's the underlying reason it took me too long to understand her subconscious penis was, in fact, compensating for something — how she felt like she possessed no control or power at all, and she just didn't know what to do anymore.

Her dreams were also warning her not to be rash: Don't move too hastily or else you'll have problems turning corners.

After learning about my pregnancy, I faced the burden of two consequential decisions: 1. What I was going to do in regard to the fetus, and 2. How I was going to tell the father. I've never dreamed of having a penis, and it showed. Maybe that's why my mother felt compelled to shoulder some of the burden, opting to tell my ex-boyfriend from earlier that year that I was pregnant, even when I asked her not to. I hadn't yet had an ultrasound, and between period spotting and an active avoidance to take accountability for my meager sexual calendar, I couldn't be certain who the father was.

Despite an ultrasound scheduled in two days, they met at a local coffee shop where she told him the news. She came back home to give me the bullet points of their conversation. The words come out too matter of fact and unapologetic. And she couldn't see past her righteousness to fully see her daughter and everything amassing inside of her. My mother just saw anger, which only solidified her decision. In reality, I was a girl afraid, stripped of a voice, and just realizing I was profoundly alone. The only option I had was to cry in my room, not realizing I was also lamenting being deprived of navigating the first important decision I faced as a teenager thrown into adulthood. This oversight eclipsed any notion I held on to that I was capable of making hard choices—that I was capable of making a choice, correct or otherwise. I was a haphazard pile crumpled on the bedroom floor. When my mother looked at me, I wonder if she opted to only see chaos over recognizing the need for a codified system to help us navigate a new and difficult space.

Maybe she was doing what she thought was best for me. We were all acting out of some kind of fear, only finding solace in the comfort of puzzle pieces, so much so, we'd often work on them late into the evening, only coming to a stopping point when our eyes were too tired to discern any potential connections. She'd say, "That's it for me," and I'd stay at the table, trying to hold on to the only thing that made me feel like I had some sense of control.

On her way to bed, my mother would tell me she'd see me in the morning. Sometimes, she'd tell me I was doing okay, and sleep would come easier that night. I'd eventually lie down on the love seat, my body curled into itself while the sexual tension between Mulder and Scully unfolded on the screen. *I want to believe* echoed in the back of my mind as I drifted off and dreamed of something whole, something bigger than the fragmented image with its missing pieces scattered across the kitchen table.

ACTing

I take the ACT eight months pregnant and refuse to get out of the chair even when Beck presses against my bladder. The numbers in the math section blur together. My reading comprehension is even worse, but I'll end up getting a 29 in English, which saves my overall score enough to get into the state university in my hometown, where I will fail after two years and a diagnosis of PTSD, anxiety, and a gnawing depression. During these two years, I will avoid home. My mother will ask to adopt Beck. Just for a little bit until your world calms, she said. But I'll refuse, perhaps because there was a small part of my brain that believed I could be the kind of mother she was when I was young. I won't factor our differences into this equation: she had my father, they were middle class, she was in her thirties, she had a home.

More bad math.

But for now I am seventeen, eight months pregnant, taking the ACT, and in desperate need of a bathroom. In two months, I'll return to school and walk with my head down in between the remaining two classes I needed to graduate: a PE credit and a sculpture class, where one student who was my friend since elementary school will call me "a fat bitch with a baby." I don't remember why, but the rest of my table shook their heads at her and no one talked for the remaining hour. We will be working on cardboard dioramas of our lives. Mine features a nasal aspirator painted black and hanging in chicken wire.

The next hour in PE, the obnoxious Republican guy from debate will tell me to go have another baby whenever I block his shot during a three-on-three basketball game. In my head, I'm confused, thinking he would have been grateful I didn't have an abortion. Out loud, I told him he wouldn't have made the shot anyway.

    I don't remember much from this time, so there's a hole in the narrative—a noticeable jump in time. Even in my thirties, I will still be working on forgiving this past self, trying to fill in the gaps.

Wall of Water

When she thought of water, she thought of how she wanted to be: bare and untouched—like a painting of a former self, a memory. She thought of Lake Michigan, which may as well have been an ocean, sand dunes rolling on the shore, the space of its water bigger than everything she had ever known, everything she would come to know. She thought of her mother, calling out from the dunes, but the girl never wanted to leave, digging her toes into the wet sand, stubborn in her contentment. She thought of what it felt like to count underwater, count to three, slowly and patiently. Her mother would laugh at this thought—the girl was never slow and patient with a single thing.

For three suspended seconds, though, the girl would be a wall of water, suspended in time. The girl would be a dispelled world, a held breath.

*

One second: The water is tall, everywhere. No one can talk to her, about her, toward her. She listens to the hum—the blue earth stilled, like giving birth in a white-walled room, if she allows herself the memory: seventeen years old, legs straddled, scared. She thought there's no turning back now. Her feet trapped in cold metal, her mother hovered over. Faces indifferent underneath clinical masks. A nurse told her, "No, honey. Don't push *that* hard," when the girl grew red in the face, forgetting to breathe after *one, two, three, push*. The nurse laughs, still floating overhead. The girl's face red from lack of oxygen and embarrassment. She wonders if grown women with husbands have made this mistake, if they've forgotten to breathe despite attending the necessary classes, did the coach speak toward them carefully, as if they were stupid, a bit slow.

*

Two seconds: The water is a mosaic of greens and blues, and she imagines herself blending into the abyss, camouflaged. Underwater, the girl forgets how her mother used to recount the story of the girl pushing too hard. After the birth, the girl's mother will tell the story to entertain, but not to be harsh, not to condescend. "In the delivery room," the mother would say, grinning, "the nurse told her not to push too hard." She snorts. "I said, 'She'll push as hard as she wants. She wanted that baby out of there.'" The girl will blush, reliving her embarrassment every time her mother recounts the image. And every time the story repeats, the girl will stretch her fingers wide, pretend there's water filling the room, blue-green hues drowning out the noise, drowning out her anticipated response when all eyes turn to her, until it floods all the holes and becomes a quiet space.

Glances like this reminded her of Lamaze class, where she always felt out of place. She was the youngest person in Lamaze, despite trying to conceal her age with subtle makeup and a modest ponytail. She corrected her posture and didn't ask questions. A pro, except when the instructor discussed the importance of your pelvic floor, and the girl blushed. "Practice your Kegel exercises daily," the instructor said. "It's an exercise you could do in a grocery store checkout line, and no one would ever know." The girl remembered hearing how Kegels were supposed to make sex feel better, and she found herself blushing harder.

*

Three Seconds: Light, just out of reach. In the water, you almost always go back up; you have to go back up. But there is always some beauty in your body rising to that first peel of water, a space where the sun reaches, its rays dancing with the tide. A decade after the birth, the girl's mother still tells the story, but instead of holding her breath, the girl looks over at her son, smiles. "That sounds like her," her son will say, laughing. He has root beer eyes—the corners curl up, mirroring a grin. His eyes remind her of damp sand, a comfortable place. Everyone chuckles, the laughter feeling like the warmth of rays just before going up for another gulp of breath. You always have to go back up, and this time, she remembers to breathe after counting to three.

*

When he smiles at her, the girl remembers how, at four, he was scared of Lake Michigan. "Don't worry," she told him. "There's a sandbar just out there, just beyond the deep parts." She pointed at the light strip lined across the lake, a refuge, a safe place for the two of them. When the water became too deep for him to walk, she told him to grab her waist, to hold on to her as she waded to the other side. And when it became too deep for her, she told him, "Grab my feet when I go underwater, and we'll dive together," just like her mother did for her as a girl, and for three seconds, they'd be in a stilled world together, the blues and greens mixing around them in a moment, bare and untouched.

Step Three

How to Be a Student

Go to college because it will make you feel like a normal teenager, like you didn't just have a baby nine months ago. Go to college to make mistakes. Go to college to confirm your sneaking suspicion you don't know anything at all. You'll learn none of us do, but you didn't have to get a degree and amass student loan debt to figure that out. This emboldens you to apply to grad school, a place designed to put you through the ringer that is equal parts existential as it is academic. You learn about Russian formalism, and you go through your first heartbreak. You teach a creative writing workshop that first fall and use a fourth of your monthly stipend to fly to Denver to say goodbye to your grandmother. A member of your cohort loses her husband to suicide, but she still makes it to the Edith Wharton conference. She will post about how she sees him in an early April snow, an image you won't be able to shake.

You'll keep wanting to learn more, and at the end of every semester, you'll worry you know less than when you started.

Galaxy Identification

Abby asks what kind of galaxy I am.

It's three in the morning, and we're nearly the lone Waffle House customers, save for a couple of drunken teenage girls avoiding going home. We're nursing dollar twenty-five coffees, hovering over notes on stars, black-holed scribbles in unlined notebooks. We've tortured ourselves with a summer astronomy lab, convincing each other we could get by with a B from last minute studying.

I try to think of galaxy options, but the teenagers are too loud for a narrow breakfast diner. I can't be too mad about it—that would have been Abby and me a handful of years ago. It could have been us just a month ago, but this summer we've replaced late-night binges with mapping star charts, trading drunken texts to unreciprocated crushes with ontological questions involving galaxy identification. Now, Abby practices yoga and paints on sprawling canvases with empty beer bottles dipped in bright acrylic. I sit on her couch, making more notebook scribbles. Sometimes, I grab my own empty beer bottle and join her. We paint on our knees, our torsos moving millions of paint layers.

I never join her for yoga because some things haven't changed, like the way I still feel clumsy next to her, uninteresting every time I move or speak. So when she asks something painfully cool—like what kind of galaxy I am—I try to give an unclumsy and interesting answer. I'm ashamed that my initial reaction is to entertain what kind of galaxy *she* is. I picture her in Adho mukha śvānāsana, her long blonde hair falling to the earth as she moves to Navasana, then Utthita Parsvakonasana, and then Garudasana. All of which is surely an elliptical galaxy, balanced with her body's weight as one limb or another is outstretched on either side.

The truth is I don't identify with a galaxy in particular, and in that sense, I still feel like a drunk teenager avoiding home. Or perhaps it's the fact I might identify with all galaxies, separate and altogether. All at once.

I want to tell her how, during moments of unrest, it's likely I will feel like an elliptical galaxy, too. But instead of embodying balance, my elliptical galaxy feels older, stretched thin. On days when I find myself with arms outstretched from existential whys, from what-the-fuck frustration, I am an elliptical galaxy. My elliptical galaxy feels more like the moments right before giving up, a fleeting instant when I still have enough energy to ask the universe: *Why me, why now, why?*

But then there's this: My arms make that same wide motion—one broad arm gasp—as I go in for an intimate hug. The kind of hug you share with close friends or family or someone new who you've just connected with intensely, and you cannot figure out how to say, "I love this moment so much," so there are your arms speaking for you. An ineffable hug. Hugs that may happen whenever I'm feeling especially moved or maybe even sad, maybe wildly happy. Perhaps it's not a matter of becoming irritable with age, but all these emotions, wonderful and terrible alike, combined in one big elliptical soup, overwhelming me and my arms to the point where I and them don't know what to do with myself or themselves, and my disjointed brain signals to my arms:

Spread   out
wide,

my whole being found in the length of two outstretched arms, whether from a hug or from flailing my limbs from the madness of rush hour traffic or the decaying world news.

I open my mouth, confident in my galaxy choice, but then I think of the Milky Way. The Milky Way—inexplicably spiraled—with too many arms winding, multiplied. Arms a corkscrew of Shiva, her hands and hands and hands twisting their way from a swelling center: a heart wanting to go everywhere, arms grasping toward all paths. I've wanted to be a neuroscientist, a surgeon, writer, a marine biologist, and anyone who studies stars. I find myself falling in love, always. I want to be a good mom and friend and daughter and sister, but I also want solitude, space. My spiraled arms reach for all things with a firm grip that only lasts so long as these arms want to grasp.

Whenever I describe my fleeting attention span to someone else, I wish I could explain it as if I were a spiral galaxy—arms interested in all the noise and pictures and people around me, all my thoughts cantering past my hippocampus's permanent open door. I worry that having too many arms will cause me to not be able to finish anything at all, and all those arms wanting to do all things—a surgeon's steady hand, a diver petting the head of a friendly octopus—will be replaced with the silence of too much space.

Spiraled galaxies contain our traces of Heidegger's nonchoices, of Frost's roads not traveled. The ghosts of this life's nonchoices follow me wherever I go: a shadow on the beaten sidewalk I walk my dog on where I think about how there are no octopuses in Missouri, an Ozarks back road I've taken too many times.

There are moments when the weight of all my choices and nonchoices can drown out everything, and I implode on myself. A neutron star is made. A death star, not quite like the one in *Star Wars*. Instead of good versus evil, a neutron star doesn't do much of anything at all. It's made of mostly neutrons, the pressure of degeneracy eventually causing the dense star to collapse and become a black hole. I wonder if I can be a black hole within a spiraled galaxy instead.

Abby asked what kind of galaxy I was either a few seconds or a billion years ago. She is quiet, waiting. She nurses on fresh coffee and her hash browns—scrambled, covered, smothered, and diced. She orders the same thing every time. And every time the waitress will look over at me, who can't decide between hash browns scattered, covered, diced, or what Abby orders. I can never remember if I like Waffle House mushrooms. What I really want is the house salad from the Italian place across the street, but it's three in the morning. The restaurant has also been closed for years.

When I ordered tonight, I got distracted by the teenagers walking through the door, so instead of any style of hash browns, I said, *A number one, please*. A number one being a cheeseburger and fries. Despite the fact I never order a cheeseburger and fries. Despite the fact I wasn't all that hungry to begin with.

Ordering food is a spiraled-galaxy moment. If I had been an irregular galaxy in this instant, I wouldn't have been at Waffle House at all. Irregular galaxies happen whenever life seems shapeless, immutable in its own presumed malformation. No distinction here. *Don't mind me — just passing by*. There are dark moments when I take on an irregular galaxy shape, times when I can't feel my throat, so I will lie in bed voiceless, arms tucked underneath. I will try to explain depression to my mother, but my throat will numb, unable to explain an incapacity to do, to be. Because even I don't understand. Maybe I'm just broken, is what I want to tell her. Maybe I'm just too different from everyone else. Irregular, no distinction. *Oops. Sorry again — just passing by*. The apology becomes a refrain for my getting in the way. Even when no one is around, I apologize to vacant air, to negative space. These are irregular-galaxied moments, moments when I attempt to make my body small, arms tucked too tight to even get in the way of themselves.

My thoughts are interrupted by laughter carrying through the diner. Maybe I was close to having an answer, perhaps the teenagers saved me from spiraling too deep.

I end up telling Abby that I don't really know what kind of galaxy I am.

It took me a few seconds, a million years, just to come up with *I don't know*. I laugh. She laughs, too, and my shoulders relax in relief.

*

On the way back to her apartment, I finally think to ask her what kind of galaxy she is.

She looks over at me as we brake toward a blinking red light. "I don't really know," she says as we make a complete stop.

Abby's answer would have been obvious if I hadn't jumped to conclusions. How could I have forgotten the way she complained about her torso being much longer than her legs? How, when she shifted into Natarajasana, the pose would demand her to focus more intently on her feet as she found balance, her left foot and her right foot, left and right arms pointing toward different directions. A spiraled galaxy all her own.

There are the times she's screamed irregular galaxy, her body folded in child's pose or maybe turtle's pose. How she tucks her hands under her knees figuring where to roll the next acrylic beer bottle. How she lies in bed after drinking too much bottom-shelf whiskey or the way she wrapped a blanket over her head whenever she thinks of men who would never love her, but men she continued to love anyway.

Aside from the flashing red light, we're alone on the street—the quiet so thick we may as well be alone in the universe.

Look, I say, pointing toward the stoplight. *A dying giant red star.*

It's winking at us from the sky, she says.

We drive past the blinking red light—past Betelgeuse, past Mira—galaxies of our own.

Hegel Exercises

1.

Stand in front of the mirror, taking your body in with question, a peanut shell—hard and hollowed—edges sharp against negative space. Notice the way your waist meets your hips, how the body opens abruptly, too wide for middle school, for high school. And they're too wide now, even as a woman. Place your hands on your hips and think about the men you've loved, the way they would place their own hands on your pelvis, fingers pressing hard against skin. In comparison, your hands feel weak, maybe too small, too feminine in contrast to their hands, hands that reach wide and grab firm, knuckles cracked, dry. Their fingerprints left white imprints on your skin when they left, but the whitened skin never stayed too long either, and you remind yourself of this as you take your hands off those hips.

Regardless of who owned the hands—perhaps it was the chef or the philosopher or the poet—regardless of any of that, they always held you the same way. And the next man will hold you the same way, too. You'll convince yourself of this while you try to fall asleep at night. And they'll all leave white marks on your already too-white skin, even if it's just for an instant, a small moment in their time with you.

Think: maybe the next man who holds my hips, the next man who runs his hands down my hips, up my hips, fingers pressing against my hips, maybe that man will do it unlike those before. Delicately but with purpose. The next man you love, things will feel different. His hands will feel different. The next man, you'll convince yourself.

2.

In his absolute idealism, Hegel offers a more hopeful historic philosophy. To communicate this dialectic, he used the German word *aufheben*, a word inherently contradictory in its definition: to sublate and to inflate, to cancel and to keep—all of these things, all at once. All in one moment.

We don't have a word for it in English, your Continental philosophy professor explained. He said, "Think of it like this: think of it like a red balloon filled to its limits, think of letting go of that balloon, hands free as the rubber escapes from you, the trapped air letting out a long fart as it escapes. Think of this happening simultaneously, the unfilling, the refilling, the unfilling again of air. That's our word for *aufheben*."

When you think of Hegel, you will always think of a long fart from a red balloon representing history. And when you think of Hegel in terms of love and relationships, you'll think of each man as a fart, too.

3.

When the first man told you he loved you, he said the words with his eyes closed loosely.

Why? you would ask.

Because you're intoxicating, a force, he said. *You're beautiful*, he said.

Ha. Ha, you said back, not a laugh.

You asked the same thing to the second man, who stared at you long and hard as he said it three times.

But he gave you the same reason—a *force, wild, enchanting*—even though he said the words differently: clear, exact.

When the third man divulged his feelings, he looked past you, into the empty space where the lines of your neck meet your shoulders. That negative space where he kissed you in the dark.

And you'd ask him why, too, but he never really gave an answer.

Because, because, he would say.

Because, he would say again, the reason fading as he pulled back your hair, grabbing the nape of your neck, kissing you where he thought you ought to be kissed. Vulnerable places.

Because? you repeated. You gave up when his lips brushed those places where you also thought you ought to be kissed.

But if the reasons are always the same, or if there was never really any reason at all, then maybe you're the sublation, the cancellation in the dialectic. Maybe you're the one who needs to do something differently, change the relationship cycle.

And how do you say *I love you* to a man? Eyes wide open, voice fading into a dimly lit room — lamps just light enough to make out the vulnerable places you've tried to hide.

4.

"Hegel doesn't want to reject or forget the past," your philosophy professor said. "*Aufheben* maintains pieces of our past, and we preserve old ideas and problems by overcoming them — that positive is only possible in the presence of negative. We're only capable of growth if we know what we are growing from."

This looks like a spiral, this preservation being raised, inflated, and he drew a long seashell on the board, the lines twisting together as he reached the top.

You thought: When do you know when you have reached the end?

And you asked: When do you know when you have reached the end?

Your professor smiled, and you felt foolish, a bit dense. "Everything has to be in place," he said. "Everything has to be in place because every part of the history we know is impartial, not altogether true — a stage, a moment in time. Hegel's end is totality, but that only happens when everything is whole, when we overcome all the stages in the developmental process. A fractal architecture.

"And we're still experiencing a partial moment. Right now. We may have solved some historical problems, answered some philosophical ideas, but our world presents itself with its own set of problems. *Aufheben*." He got excited saying the word. "*Aufheben!*"

A partial instant right there in the classroom: unfilled and refilled to the brim.

5.

Go on dates with different men. Imagine how they would say *I love you*. Wonder if they are too serious, too analytic. Like the philosophy student you knew during your undergraduate days, who would talk to you after class about the content—Heidegger, Derrida, Foucault. But the Continental stuff makes you sleepy, and this is discouraging to men who love philosophy.

Head already spinning from the lecture, you'd listen with a weak smile, nodding absently. Or maybe these potential lovers would be more like the poet, who didn't make your head spin. Rather, he'd hardly talk about anything at all—cryptic in his words, his actions, who repeated, *Because, because*, but knew where to kiss you. Then there was the chef who was enthusiastic, positive, who talked the right amount for your jumbled head. You found problems there, too. He wasn't deep, and you found yourself thinking back to the philosopher. It made you feel uneasy when your mind ached for convolution. Maybe you'll never know what you want. Even now, you're nowhere near closer to understanding Hegelian totality. Not even a little bit.

Talk to different men. If you kiss, notice the way they feel differently inside of you, how you felt differently outside of yourself with each one. Sleep with them if you feel safe, or sleep with them if you're feeling reckless. A sexual *aufheben* of your own. The unfilling, refilling, and unfilling. And even when you think you're ready for a new stage (HA! You mean man!), you will still feel unfilled more than anything else. You'll want to ask yourself what's the opposite of a Hegelian dialectic.

Perhaps you're devolving. Perhaps you should go on more dates with women.

Or what happens when there is more deflating over inflating? What if you're altogether deflated—do you start from the beginning then?

But smile when you think about Hegel exercises. Make a joke to people about *aufheben*-ing your vagina and the dialectic of dating. People find this more captivating than the ability to comprehend Hegelian dialectics.

6.

When you were seventeen, you attended a class on Kegel exercises with your baby's father, who wanted to go despite the fact that the two of you weren't together. "It's for the baby," he said. "It's for Beck." But you still found that your breath got a little heavier and your heart faster when you heard the name of the son you hadn't yet met. It had been nine years since you told your mother you wanted to be a mom when you grew up. You don't know when the answer changed, but you worried that your lack of maternal desire would impact your ability to nurture a child. There were other factors, too, like the fact that he was a mild-mannered conservative Christian while you boasted your liberalism in high school debate class. You went to church for your mother, but you told your friends you were an apathetic agnostic. You were never mild-mannered enough, and you worried that, between the three-year age difference and the disparity of natures, your ex was better built to be a good parent. A part of you worried that perhaps this would mean he'd love your son more, too.

7.

Sometimes you'll wake up to different doors on nights you don't have your son. Even though these doors are only five steps away, nothing ever felt further away. He sleeps too soundly beside you. Just get to the door. One step, two, three, four steps, five steps away.

Later, he'll shift his weight in bed, placing his arms on your empty space. You wonder if he'll wake when he can't find your hips. Or worse: you wonder if he won't notice anything missing at all.

Why did you leave? he might ask the next day.

Because, because.

You'll never give him the real reason—how you're scared after the last abrupt breakup, which also broke your son's heart. A friend tells you that you'll never move forward if you linger in the past. You never bring your son around these men. You won't even mention their names.

8.

In Hegel's Master-Slave dialectic, Hegel discusses the need for recognition of the self-consciousness and what happens when two individuals confront each other. Your professor said that when one self-consciousness meets another self-consciousness, it's like looking at yourself. Like a mirror in each person's hands, any kind of hands, too. And the self-consciousness sees itself in the mirror, but it also sees its own reflection from holding its own mirror, reflecting itself, ad infinitum.

This paralyzes you with confusion and bewilderment. It paralyzes the other with confusion and bewilderment, too: a party of two self-consciousnesses feeling self-conscious, a bag of unfilled red balloons at their sides.

To recognize the other, you must also recognize yourself.

Hegel says the only way to overcome this mirroring problem is to take action, a metaphorical fight, when one must defeat the other, a master and slave. *Because, because.*

But the contradiction is this: neither the master nor the slave achieves absolute knowledge, Hegel's end goal, in this relationship. It's inherently asymmetrical, the slave's mirror showing his master's face, self-consciousness defeated.

9.

Look in the mirror again for just an instant—your body, your being—both sublated and inflated, all at once, in that moment. Wonder if your next phase, the next man who says he loves you, would look better if, rather than looking toward each other, you both gazed out in the same direction, a unifying whole. So you stop staying the night where a door is five steps too far, and you'll start breathing in and out, but not at the same time because then you'll die or combust. You won't focus on your hips or how you'll say I love you. You won't look into the mirror too long.

Count the Beats

I find myself on rough back roads that twist away toward something new, something unknown. I know them like the back of my throat, I know how far they can take me away from my pot-selling neighbors and the man with a ripped jean jacket hanging loose over a stained gray shirt. He offers to cut my grass in the summer and spring, and I tell him, *No, I can do it. No, my boyfriend will be back from school soon.* While I wait, the back roads will call me out of my small house with black mold and a depressed dog. They beckon me to leave my blank-faced, four-walled structure, complete with watered-down shampoo bottles and yellow notices from the electric company reading FINAL NOTICE. I'll never call it home.

I'll live alone here after Paul moves to Boston to get a doctorate in philosophy because he wanted to better understand the difference between being versus Being versus be-ing. When he takes a course on Heidegger and love, he will call to ask what it means when someone says they love you—in particular, what I meant when I told him I loved him. I tell him it means I care about him, that we make each other's lives better. *But what does it mean ontologically?* he asks. I'm already tired from speculation.

We have been together for four years, but I don't tell him how it feels different now, how, when I say "I love you," the words kind of fall out of my mouth and hang in the air, like recently forgotten memory. But he wouldn't be able to sense this over a phone, a lag in a Skype call.

What does Heidegger mean when he says he loves you? What does Boston mean to you?

Or your small apartment with no living room, a futon mattress for a bed? I want to ask back.

I don't know how long it takes to get to a country road when you live in Boston, and I will think of this the first and last time I visit Paul. What I do know: The point where the outskirts of Ozark suburbs turn into trailer parks, mothers calling children to come inside for supper, where the mailboxes turn from dark metal to plastic fish, mouths open for bill notices and Christmas cards from relatives far away, relatives nearly removed. Here, the land is wetter, and the people talk slower, but only so you don't miss a word, don't miss a beat. Here, the road is patched with different hues of gray cement, different hues of gray hair on men who wave to whoever is passing through, whether it be a girl with a sad dog or someone with purpose, someone who has a reason to drive down these roads.

No matter where you go, the wind is stronger here, barreling through dead oak trees and bales of hay speckled across acres of land. Where the county lines become larger and farther apart, the neighbors become few and far between, and that wind carries through them without asking names.

Just to the west of my house are blinking cows and Civil War ghosts, the bunch of them stranded on worn hills. When I drive past them, they ask, *Why are you driving so fast? Where do you need to get to so soon?* The cows and I, these soldiers, we all know the pastures and where the Ozark Mountains begin to bud in southwest Missouri. We've memorized the places where honeysuckle grows thick, a wall of yellow and white along the roads, and the air's sweetness seeps into open windows, traveling with you on the pavement. And when you pass through a tunnel of trees, sunrays fall through maple-leaved gaps. They tattoo the roads with light.

Unlike me, the cows and Civil War ghosts can't venture far enough to know the turns of the road or where the palominos stand by a barbed-wire fence, flicking flies off one another's faces. They can't see the house by the drying mouth of the James River, the house where I took piano lessons, my teacher saying over and over, *Count the beats, girl. Count the beats.* I know these back roads like the beats of *Für Elise* or the Ukrainian Carol—my father's favorite songs, but songs he never heard me play at recitals, and I sat waiting, alone on a bench, my fingers like rural county lines. I can hear the beat of my teacher's voice echoing down her yellow hallway lined with a photographic history of her family, save the photos of her ex-husband she took down during my second year of lessons.

I know these back roads like the music under my skin, whether counting the beats on a piano or the fading FM signals as you go farther north, where some of the roads turn to dead ends and the teenagers smoke pot, and there's nothing but foreclosed land and turkey vultures eating roadkill. Where there's nothing but my fingers tapping to the beats. My west is full of loud music, fast-paced beats to dim out the braking light of sunset. Loud music can dim out the idea of going back east toward my house and its mold, back toward the dull city wind.

I can tell which back roads lead to meth labs and which ones will take me to a bend in the river where it's deep enough to swing off a rope, head rolled back so far all you can see is the sky and the limbs of the trees until you hit the face of the water, making you cough when you meet back up with the all-embracing air.

Some of the back roads in the north lead to semitrucks barreling down highways toward bigger cities without plastic fish mailboxes, and some bring you to gas stations with fried foods, the cashier bored from lottery ticket sales and refilling cigarette dispensers. When I stop for a soda, narrowed eyes tell me to go back home, back toward the suburbs with stability, consistency, new bridges and paved roads. Arched eyebrows tell me dogs don't have clinical depression, and neither do people.

But my house has black mold, I want to tell them, *just like you and everyone you know.* My house makes me sick, makes my brain muddled. I'm slow on the uptake. It makes it hard to breathe, but the wind around this gas station makes it easier. Even your fried food is easier on my lungs. Perhaps I don't want to sit in this house because it reminds me of the houses that came before it, any house that followed the home with Alternanthera and an elephant boulder. I can't remember a time before disconnection notices for unpaid utilities—the pink paper is seared into me. Even my shower reminds me of my mother's shower. I've taken on her habit of watering down shampoo until I convince myself I can afford a new bottle.

Please talk slow and simple to me, I want to ask them, exhausted by Heideggerian romantic obfuscation. The only thing I understand is the wind and slow talkers and counting the beats to only the songs I care to know.

But I don't ask, so I go farther north toward the dying bridge, which creaks like my head when my ex-boyfriend tried to talk to me about Heidegger and love, where a black-haired girl hung herself, and you can see her ghost after midnight if you stop your car in the middle and count to three. I tried once, a decade ago, in the dead of winter, but she didn't come. Just me, in the middle of a bridge, telling her maybe we'll beat these teenage blues. Count to three, focus on your breath.

The winter here is different. Ice falls until the branches become too heavy and crash down onto power lines. The electricity will go out, even if you've paid it on time. Even in the cold months, I prefer the half-paved back roads to sitting in my house that runs cold with the furnace on high. Next winter, I'll light two dozen candles and line them along my coffee table just to keep warm.

Before the house, before Boston, Paul and I lived in a small apartment on the cusp of downtown Springfield. During our junior year of undergrad, we woke to a rare Missouri whiteout. For thirty minutes, we stood in the doorway, staring into the white, our faces cold and backs warm.

I tell him I've never seen snow like this before.

Too tall, he bends awkwardly to kiss my forehead. *Then don't forget it*, he tells me and walks back inside. I don't follow him back in—just stand there watching, drifting with the flakes. I won't forget the snow, but I won't remember what came next. Perhaps we walked down to the corner bar with other brave friends. Did we make love when the electricity went out? Did the electricity even go out.

I seldom go east, where my father built an engineering plant to make activated carbon. There is a hole in the basement of the building, and as a child I thought it didn't end, that if I fell into it, no one could ever help me back up. The back roads here smell like forgotten slaughterhouses, where piglets cry for their long-gone mother and a father they never knew. There was a slaughterhouse just on the other side of the plant, and my father told me once in a hushed tone, a tone I only remember him using once, that if we were quiet enough, you could hear swine ghosts calling out through broken windows.

What I don't remember: how my parents took out a large loan together to get the business started or how it failed because he didn't love her anymore. When they separate, I found myself dreaming of the abandoned slaughterhouse next door. I can smell the aftermath of pigs dying, beaten alive and crying for someone, whoever would hear. Their fathers were gone, their mothers lost. I still have dreams about the hole at the end of the stairs, how, when I reach the bottom, I plunge in without looking back, falling forward, indefinitely. The ground is wet, and it smells like burnt bacon.

The plant is now a meth lab. I drove by, stopped, and the air still smelled like a slaughterhouse but with a chemical breeze. But I don't have the heart to tell this to my father, who still loves to dream, beating a dead pig with superior carbon. I don't tell him despite missed piano recitals, missed beats, missing family portraits from my mother's hallway.

Before my father's plant, Paul and I had known each other. His father, a chemist, my father, an engineer, had worked together producing pharmaceuticals to make you feel better, to make you feel less pain. The men played darts on Saturdays while my mother cut his mother's hair. Paul and I were left to play in the backyard.

A standstill in time: six-year-old me says, smiling to Paul, *Did you know if you stare at the sun long enough and look away, it will turn the world green?*

How long is long enough? Paul is four but already showing an inclination for deeper questions.

We crossed paths again while both studying philosophy, and he followed me around for a year, trying to get me to go on a date, trying to get me to show him the world turned green again. But even with the sun out, my earth felt opaque. The dusty film didn't clear in my head until the back roads, until the sunlight-splashed hills and honeysuckled walls.

I don't go to the south if I'm alone. The back roads there are too tangled, too much to dissect, to understand well. The back roads there are the back of my throat, dry from the wind blowing over my voice, an unnamed man grabbing the roots of my hair, telling me *I'm not fourteen if it's too dark to see.*

Even when the fireflies are out, the south feels off. Its anxiety carries with me back home, when I'm too anxious to count my breath like my counselor told me to do when I was feeling anxious as a teenager. It carries with me back to my relationships, where I'll still cry if Paul touches me a certain way, if he grabs my wrists while having sex or pulls my hair too hard.

The slowest drives are the ones back to the center of everything, back to the black mold, my dog—head cocked—asking, *Where have you been? Why do you look so sad?*

On the way back, the beats get softer but more heavy-handed, the oaks, cows, the soldiers all calling me home. Instead, I go back to the place where I wanted to tell my ex, phone dying in hand, that Heidegger would say love is about the choices we make and the choices we do not make, and how, alone in this house, maybe love would be better if tossed to the wind rolling across county and state lines that divide everything we used to know, everything we used to love.

Unbreaking an Egg

In 2019, Beck is too tall. I ask him to stop growing already. My thirteen-year-old tells me to relax, that time is a construct, and we laugh the same laugh we laugh whenever we call anything a construct. Our low chuckles will fade out the car window or hang in the negative space between television sets and living room furniture. In this instance, we are sitting across from each other at a Vietnamese restaurant. Our laughter dissolves into the noise of a blender grinding.

He looks down at his phone, eyebrows narrow and too serious. In the span of a moment, he looks like a grown human. I take a mental snapshot, something I do when an image or feeling is so striking that I cognitively file it away—something to return to later. Mental snapshots are holding time in cupped hands, memories like water trying to seep past the cracks between your fingers.

But my mind often feels tired between the outer world and my own interiority, struggling to feel peace in environments not designed for people who aren't neurotypical. My late diagnosis of ADHD–inattentive type has helped me understand the roots of a life saturated with anxiety, a life of fast heart rates, perpetually flushed cheeks, and the need for five drinks to create the illusion of comfort in whatever given social dynamic.

The diagnosis also came with an underactive prefrontal cortex (PFC), creating dog-shit executive functioning. The PFC regulates working memory, which explains why mental snapshots are dripping through my fingers, draining hand-cupped time.

There's another thing. I've had an increase in striking moments turned mental photographs in the last couple of years. The truth is, the growth is causing the pool of snapshots to spill past my memory's grip, and sometimes the moments blend together.

The bad bleeds together, too. I've been avoiding talking about me as I was ten years ago because my present self has made a lot of effort to not look back. When I started researching for a piece for Past Ten, a writing project that solicits reflections from writers on who they were ten years earlier, there was a small shyness in the nostalgia, as if my Facebook history was somehow a physical manifestation of my 2009 self: twenty-one years old and unable to see opportunity beyond working as a credit card sales adviser for a bank too big to value its entry-level employees. September 4 that year fell on a Friday, which means I worked a ten-hour day/ spent ten hours distracting myself from answering customer service calls.

More often than not, I would avoid going home after work, but I don't think that was the case ten years ago. There are two Facebook posts proving September 4, 2009, to be an extra ontologically heavy day.

Status one reads:

is pretty much done.

Status two:

Be

I want to clarify with my 2009 self what she meant by "Be," but I'm the only one in 2009 or 2019 who can answer that. I suppose I should take the post's advice and just let it be. Instead, I spend a moment with a previous self, scrolling past September 2019 to see what kind of ruckus I was up to. It turns out she wasn't all that bad—just needed some grounding, some time with herself even though she tries her best to avoid being alone.

It's really a bit funny—the fear of returning, of being shy around one's self. When I first thought about who I was in 2009, I immediately polarized my two selves, brushing aside who I was ten years ago because I wasn't proud of her, of where she wasn't going. I think all that really means is that I didn't possess enough patience and self-love for whatever version of self I'm looking at/am/etc.

The biggest difference is I now know my brain a little more intimately, helping me understand the reason why I navigate the world the way I do. I have tools to work toward a semblance of a future, whereas my twenty-one-year-old self couldn't imagine where she would be in a few seconds, or eight days. A million years.

2009 Facebook posts reveal what we have in common: a love for overcast days and fresh rain on asphalt, the way Beck makes us so happy. Both versions an attempt to hold memories in cupped hands—some hope to return to whenever the world feels too difficult to navigate.

*

If time is a construct, my younger self is out there now.

In ten years, a friend will explain nonlinear time to her—research for an essay looking at where she was a decade ago. The friend will talk about the absence of causality in nonlinear time, so it allows for certain impossibilities. "Like if you could unbreak an egg," he will say.

And for a moment, she'll wonder if she can become unbroken like an egg. Her mind will swirl in the thought for only a small moment—a few seconds, a million years—just long enough to realize the possibility was already there.

A Scattering of Our Own

In the midst of sorrow, sickness, death, or misfortune of any kind, and in the presence of the notable and great, silence was the mark of respect. More powerful than words was silence with the Lakota.

—Chief Luther Standing Bear, Oglala Sioux Tribe

In the holes we fill during silence, the earth speaks, a low hum where we find ourselves again. But it is before this silence when we may lose ourselves, perhaps lose one another, forgetting our names until driving with the windows down or breathing in the moment when we spread the last bit of someone loved. David reaches silence in the book of Psalms, waiting for God, waiting for salvation. In Buddhism, silence achieves whole mind, mouths unable to interfere with pure consciousness. Trappist monks uphold the virtue of silence in order to express isolation within a community, separate but together.

A man who visited a Benedictine monastery in New Mexico talked about his vow of silence. A cacophony, really. He said you can hear your body if you listen, head bowed, hands folded on the rivets of your hard skull. The biggest silence is the desert and sky molding together into nothingness, bare and untouched. The biggest silence of all, he explained, is death.

*

The Lakota word *Oglala* is translated as "to scatter one's own," stemming from the six tribes separating to provide protection against outside tribes and white settlers. With time, the scattering of their own blurred the edges of the Sioux culture, giving birth to a thinner bloodline, descendants removed bit by bit. Descendants like my paternal grandmother, a woman who was taught to overlook those pieces of herself, pieces her mother couldn't connect to and her father wasn't present to pass on. Despite these things being forgotten, my grandmother, not recognizing it, carried on Lakota tradition with her unshakable pride and an unyielding value of family. Her ancestors breathed through her storytelling, tales expressed with both laughter and hands. For more than fifty years, the Lakota spirits nodded, firm and steady, whenever my grandmother kept my grandfather balanced with a deeply rooted heel, reminding him to drink iced Bud Light instead of dark liquor.

But the balls of her feet collapsed after a series of strokes one early September, her biopsy results showing late stages of pancreatic cancer. The doctor gave her two months, maybe until Thanksgiving.

*

Tomorrow is Halloween. I landed in Denver three hours and four glasses of pinot noir ago, but my grandfather is set on shifting the focus from the slow breaths on the baby monitor to someone else's future, someone outside of this home where future implies something, anything. While we wait for Maa to waken, he tries to convince me to submit a story to *Playboy*'s contest for college writers.

"I've read some winners in the past, and I figured someone in the family could do better."

He says this three times over the course of fifteen minutes, as if rehearsed. As if the sentence could deter the things left unspoken, the quiet moments when the baby monitor coughs, and his eyebrows narrow deeper.

He says it again: "I think you could do it." The whites of his eyes become even more still, and though I have never sent him or my grandmother or my father or my Aunt Jill any of my stories, I pretend he means it.

The plane ride has made me withdrawn, awkward to speech. When I close my eyes, I can only see the edges of Missouri, the tops of its deciduous trees like dead broccoli crowns from the sky. When my lids open, my grandfather's mouth continues to move, making different shapes of Kansas agronomy as he talks faster about the *Playboy* contest. He refills our glasses of pinot noir, avoiding the iced Bud Light that makes him ache.

"Go for it, kiddo," Aunt Jill says, taking a sip of a Corona.

"Why not?" I smile, and I nod. I say, "I'll do it," knowing I may forget under the weight of student projects to grade, essays discussing burkas in Pakistan or Botswanan Bushmen holding hands, stroking the hairs on their neighbor's arms. I've told my students: "Try to understand Other—don't be so closed off." I say to my family, "Okay, I'll do it," aware I could get caught up on my seminar class transcribing Civil War letters written by forgotten names—forgotten lovers and brothers, sons and friends.

And my grandfather and aunt know it, too. I can tell by the way he tightens his crinkled eyelids. The way she looks down at her Corona bottle—smile weak, eyes closed.

Even still, I go to the basement to study, research that consists of flipping through decades of *Playboys* stored on the bookshelf by the pool table. Back in '96, my grandfather had my brother and me organize them in chronological order, starting with the March 1978 issue featuring "Ralph Nader on Sports" and an interview with Bob Dylan. Also, Debra Jensen's breasts.

When my brother and I got to the summer of 1985, my grandmother came downstairs in her eggplant-hued sweatpants and gasped when she saw my brother holding June—the cover featuring Roxanne Pulitzer wearing a blue-sequined leotard and carrying a brassy trumpet, the pages dancing back and forth as he thumbed through.

She paused at the foot of the stairs, turning sharply toward my grandfather. "For Pete's sake, Pa. What in God's name are you having them do?"

My brother was mortified—red faced, guilty. My grandfather laughed, saying something about how she wanted him to clean up the bookshelf. She joined in, and, just like it always did, her laughter overpowered his with both infectiousness and strength. Their laughter echoed up the stairs, carrying through the entire home.

If Maa could make it to the basement now to see me researching past *Playboy* stories, overwhelmed by nipples and an excerpt from Lydia Davis, she would still laugh, even though it may hurt.

Back upstairs, my grandfather is sautéing garlic, another glass of pinot noir within reach. I take a seat next to Jill, who's still at the kitchen bar drinking her Corona, splashing more lime juice in the bottle every few sips.

Gramps says, "The uncertainty is the worst. The not knowing is the worst."

Jill says, "I wake up three or four times a night just to see if I can hear the baby monitor. If she's still breathing."

I say nothing, shifting my weight on the barstool. I say nothing because I live in Missouri, in the lukewarm heart of the Ozarks, where the soft mountains look like goose bumps in comparison to the sharp angles of the Rockies. I say nothing because I am far away even now, a disconnected niece who has neglected the Lakota value of family, a granddaughter who hurries through phone calls with her grandparents. Because I am a person who does not yet understand the Trappists' awareness of separate but together.

*

Standing Bear explains Wakan Tanka, the Great Spirit, and how it breathed life and motion into all things, both visible and invisible. This spirit was over all, through all, and in all. It was great as the sun, and it was good as the earth. Nothing surpassed the greatness and goodness of the Big Holy. The Lakota could not look at nothing without looking at Wakan Tanka, and one could not evade its presence, for it pervaded all things and filled all space.

In the holes we fill during silence, the earth speaks, the low hum of Wakan Tanka pushing us to remember our names and balance ourselves when we find ourselves lost.

When I thought I had nothing to say to my grandfather and Jill, I should have said: Maa's laughter is Wakan Tanka, permeating through everything and everyone.

*

When the low breathing on the baby monitor turns to stark coughs and the whispers of a name, my grandfather and Jill leave the kitchen to check on my grandmother. I sit still and unknowing, unsure if I should help or if I will only get in the way of a hardened routine.

Instead, I pace around, breathing in the home's history. A photographic evolution of Jill's son and daughter, children with stronger noses and a darker complexion, flood the refrigerator door. In my grandfather's office, drawings done by near and distant cousins cover the wall lined with sunlight between blinds. Illustrations of flowers and epistolary comments ending with their love, forever.

Above his computer are my brother's and my school portraits from 1997. We're both smiling widely, blond haired and light eyed. Our mother's Swedish blood seeping out of our pores.

'97. The same year Dad left Mom, the year I stopped coming to see the Rockies as often.

And as this realization flashes throughout my mind, I begin to wonder if my grandfather ever looks up from his work, remembering the time we organized *Playboy* magazines on the blue felt of the pool table. Remembering how Maa's laugh echoed up the stairs where now there is only low baby monitor breaths and silence.

Wherever I go, I can hear the conversation on the baby monitor.

"Did you have her swish today, Dad?" Jill asks.

"I gave her Tylenol. No swish."

"I'll get her up, Dad. You just stay there."

"Okay," he says, his voice mechanical but inconsistent in strength.

Then there are the just audible responses of my grandmother. Unsure responses. Responses in pain and discomfort. Disquieted responses. Responses in her home, in a cot, her limbs wrapped around my aunt while being placed in a wheelchair.

I walk in as Jill lifts a foot onto each rest, ankles angled unnaturally.

I say, "Hi, Maa. I'm here. I'm so happy to be here." The words are saturated with that awkward speech.

*

A call from Dad: Sorry I can't be in Colorado with you. Have to catch a flight for work tomorrow. Remember that this will be a quiet trip. She still has a bit of humor. You can still see parts of her. But she hardly ate when I was there last week: a bite or two of fish, a shot of Ensure. Nothing the last two days. There is a lot of waiting.

When she gets up, appreciate it. She will only want to be out of bed for twenty, maybe thirty minutes. She'll smoke half a cigarette or so, take a few sips of beer.

*

I see the changes in her body more clearly the next day, the morning light making her look smaller underneath her fleece blanket decorated with wolves howling at the moon. She wears her golfing cap, eyes steady underneath. Maa smokes her Misty 120 with her left hand, her good side, as she looks beyond the backyard fence. Jill watches her, then she watches Gramps hovering over her with his body and his questions.

Gramps asks, "Do you want more of that cod? A few more shots of Ensure? Do you want to stay up later and watch the trick-or-treaters?"

Jill says, "Give her a break."

Maa says, "No, no—too tired," with an eye roll and a soft shake of the head, but there is a hint of a grin at the left corners of her lips, a small smile my grandfather doesn't catch as he puts out the rest of her half-smoked Misty in the ashtray.

I move forward in time—a week, maybe a month—and picture him struggling to toss the partial Misties away, wondering how long it will take for him to throw them out once she is gone. Will it be fast, all at once? Or will he throw them out bit by bit? If the latter, will he finger the edges of the cigarette where her mouth once was, sucking in the smoke and thinking back to the first time they kissed in a mountain bar, music buzzing while they leaned against the pool table?

Maa asks me questions, slow and quiet. I tell her about graduate school and teaching, how it's demanding, but I'm learning so much. I mention the Civil War letters I'm transcribing for my linguistics seminar, how Sergeant Charles Lutz wrote to his brother every week, his letters asking him to look after the rest of the family, letters saying how he heard the war would be over soon, letters always ending with his love sent. I tell her about how the shape of love's *L* and the curl of the *C* in his name are imprinted in my brain.

"It's like I know him," I say to her.

She shakes her head—slow and sad—looking up to the mountains.

*

The Medicine Wheel, a circle with a cross, holds great significance for the Oglala Sioux, the circle representing a ceaseless pattern of life through death and the cross creating four distinct directions of Being. These directions are marked by a color to demonstrate these paths, and, in the center, Wakan Tanka balances all things through connectedness.

In the east, the yellow sun gives light to all of the Great Spirit's creations; it generates new beginnings. When wisdom and growth are needed, they look to the white north to bring guidance, while the west offers introspection through the black solitude. Life begins in the south, marked by red to embody life after death.

The south signifies the move into Wanagi Makoce, the neutral spirit land. As a Sioux Indian nears this death, the tribe paints her face red with vermillion, a symbol of smooth transition into her next phase of life.

*

Maa is sleeping longer. Jill wakes her once at noon to have her swoosh, rinsing her mouth to prevent sores, and then she goes back to bed. At five, she wants a cigarette and a sip of iced Bud Light.

Outside, my grandfather asks her again about watching the trick-or-treaters, and he clenches his jaws, eyebrows slightly raised, when she surprises us with a nod.

In his relief, he starts talking fast, uncontrolled. He prattles on about Halloween when Jill and Dad were young, how the cousins would come over and the neighborhood would be full of kids. He reminds her how

Zuni Street was still full of kids even though a lot of them were from that apartment filled with Mexicans, but it made everything more colorful, more alive.

Changing direction, he talks about the last time we all played asshole, her favorite card game, while she bit the edges of Rainier cherries and spit the seeds into her empty can of Bud Light. How, when she finally won a hand, she yelled with her mouth and her hands, "Me! I'm El Presidente, and you're the asshole, Pa! El Presidente," emphasizing every letter in the word, and how much he loved that she emphasized every letter of the word, and he speaks quicker with every word like he wants to breathe her all in at once and not ever let her go back to bed, face bare or painted.

*

After the last of the trick-or-treaters, she's ready to go back to sleep.

"I did good," Maa says to us.

"You did good," Jill says.

I smile. I nod back.

Later, when the breaths on the baby monitor falter, my grandfather doesn't move, doesn't speak, until the breathing becomes again.

"I think it's time for bed," he says, and he goes downstairs, walking past the pool table, past the *Playboys*.

*

When I say my goodbyes, I tell my grandfather that I'll write the *Playboy* story, and perhaps I will after saying it a second time. I tell Jill thank you. To my grandmother: I love her, I will try to call more. How I will see her on Thanksgiving.

"Love ya, love ya, love ya," Maa says, the word *love* always strong even though it may hurt to say it louder. Even though she must say it three times—always three times.

"She may not make it until Thanksgiving," my father tells me on the phone.

"She may not make it until the end of this week," my grandfather says.

*

On the flight back home, I try not to think about Thanksgiving or leaving Colorado, away from these mountains, away from the slowing breaths on baby monitors or the memories my grandfather is holding tight, fists clenched firm. Next to me is a tall, handsome boy in dirtied cowboy boots who doesn't say a word until we are up in the air.

"Jeez, I'll be damned," he says. "Look at all those clouds. Seems like we'll never get out."

I nod, and I smile, just like I do moments later when he asks if he can read me a poem he has just written on our journey, counting syllables on his left hand and shaking his boots when something isn't right.

As he reads me the poem, I drown out the images of horses and evergreen trees. His voice blurs into the hiss of the air conditioner, and as he fades, all I can think about is the whiteness of the clouds and the whiteness of the wings of the plane and the whiteness of my thoughts, wondering if that's what the edges of a clock, the blurred edges of time, look like against the blankets of our own eyelids.

And this is all I can do because I don't want to imagine how the smile of a rugged poet I met on a plane ride is more convincing than me telling her, "Love you, Maa. I'll call when I get back home."

*

The Lakota uphold the body as a temple for the spirit, a place that must not be disturbed in order to fulfill the next transition to the neutral spirit land. Because of this, the tribe chooses to have burials rather than cremate the body. In the Keeping of the Souls ritual, the body is dressed in fine clothing and ornaments. The grieving family takes a lock of their loved one's hair, tucking it into a buckskin cloth, where her soul will live in a sacred place in their tepee. In a year, the celebration of Wanagi Yuha allows the purified soul to be released, while the tribe commemorates the spirit through stories and gifts.

In the beginning of the ritual, the Shaman says to the mourners:

You are now keeping the soul of your own loved one, who is not dead, but is with you. From now on you must live in a sacred manner, for your loved one will be in this tepee until her soul is released. You should remember that the habits which you establish during this period will remain with you always. Your hands are holy; treat them as such! And your eyes are holy; every day and night your loved one will be with you; look after her soul all the time, for through this you will always remember Wakan Tanka.

*

On Thanksgiving, my father and brother stare out the car windows, the Rockies filling all the space. The Rockies Wakan Tanka.

When I consider spreading her ashes, a knot in my stomach grows with the question of how far she will drift down into the town of Golden, wondering if any of the unknowing people will breathe some of her in as they pass by: a bit of her laugh, her love for iced Bud Light. Her pride, her cheekbones.

On top of Mount Zion, we head up the walkway leading to the *M* made of white stones. The *M* represents the School of Mines, the college both my father and aunt went to, each of them carrying their own white rock their freshman year to build on the tradition. Here, she will go south on the Medicine Wheel, her wisdom keeping my grandfather balanced when he looks to the *M* on his morning walks. Perhaps he will feel like David and find a new salvation under the weight of silence.

We take turns carrying her up the mountain, her body only a few pounds of dusty bones held in a plastic bag. The Colorado air is thin but heavy with what is unsaid. At the bottom of the *M*, we wait for my grandfather to speak, and he falters several times before finding a solid ground of resolve.

In the paused stillness, we pass her around, saying something small in an even smaller voice.

We pour her out bit by bit. A scattering of our own.

When it is my turn to speak, I say *I love you* with my jaws tight and head bowed, ashamed at the brevity. What I really mean to say is: I love you now like I love the desert. Untouchable, bare. I love you like Wakan

Tanka, like the Rocky Mountains and the open sky molding into one another, into nothing and everything all at once.

*

With each pour, the sky fills with you, the wind not knowing what direction to take. I feel your body, your laughter filling all space in the silence. A cacophony, really. You don't float down toward the busy people below, up their noses or into their foamy lattes. Instead, the wind carries you into our own nostrils, into our own mouths. But this doesn't stir a knot in my stomach or cause a cringe in my side. You're simply there, continuing in us all: in our tightened throats, the corners of our eyes and lungs.

When you have come full circle, you're back in his hands one more time before he lets that last bit go. And he stares at you hard as he waves the bag up and down and north and south and to the sun and to the earth, until your dust, a film of everything we knew, is gone.

When he is finished, he holds onto that empty plastic bag, looking at it like he could just put it in his pocket, like he could take it with him anywhere he went.

*

On the drive back, my grandfather tells me that this, that everything, was endearing, repeating the word slowly and purposefully—*endearing, endearing*—with a gasp of a smile in between syllables. He shakes his head in disbelief, as if no word in any other language could have been more fitting. *Endearing.* He rolls down the car window, waving his hand in the cold mountain air, saying it again. *How endearing, how endearing,* the words pouring into the all-embracing silence.

Step Four

How to Untangle Knots

Use detangler spray and one of your wide-tooth combs you've amassed from times you thought they were lost. Turns out you had them all along, you just didn't have a place to call home, your life lacking continuity and consistency. Just know: in a handful of years, you will have five wide-tooth combs, and you will have a place to call home. Give thanks.

Start from the bottom and work your way up, the only way you can go. Let yourself cry, and remember what your mother said about the necklaces you left at the bottom of your drawers: "Every knot can be undone." She said something about patience, too, which you were never good at. Something you got from her.

Eventually all of your knots will become undone, and you'll feel human again. You'll seldom think of the man from grad school who broke you in two, who caused your life to feel desperately tangled. You wish you could visit this former self to let her know all the good things she has coming, but for now: learn patience and untangle knots.

One Fish, Two Fish

There were two fish left in his aquarium—an emerald green corydoras and a red-tailed black shark. Their home was a fifty-five-gallon tank that took up too much space in his small one-bedroom apartment on the east side of town. He would never get rid of the tank, he told me. A family heirloom, and he's a quiet, sentimental kind. Though on the surface, you'd never think it, with his barrel chest and the red beard hanging two inches below his jaw. He smoked his cigarettes in long breaths while he was short winded in conversations. Unless you got a few whiskey and Cokes in him. Then he'd open up, drink by drink.

This is how I got to know him—in a dimly lit bar where blue-collar workers came in after their shifts. Mostly men who worked at the Kraft plant down the road, a phantom scent of plastic cheese from my childhood hovering in the air.

His laughter was too loud after the fifth whiskey and Coke. Eyebrows were more animated. *Like mine*, I thought, sipping on my own drink—whiskey neat. *It's better that way.*

Easier to read a lie.

He talked about his mom being an alcoholic, how she'd embarrassed him when he traveled back home, a small town a hundred and fifty miles northeast of Springfield. He read me a poem, but I didn't hear him mention the name, and I forgot once he started. I liked the way he read, how he didn't miss a beat and how his quiet demeanor came across as loyal to the text rather than masturbatory to his voice. He paused at the end of each stanza, stared at it hard. Eyebrow thoughtful.

He talked about his dog, an American Eskimo dog, he told me. "He's an asshole. Stubborn." The sentence was matter of fact but not judgmental. I thought perhaps he identified.

"Assholes are okay," I said. I could feel my cheeks getting rosy, and I wasn't sure whether it was from the whiskey or a response to how he looked into me—firm and purposeful.

"My fish aren't assholes," he said. He smiled. "Well, maybe the red-tailed black shark."

"There's a little asshole in all of us," I said, finishing my drink. Too much. The overload of whiskey in my throat burned, and he laughed when I shook my head back and forth quickly, as if it would weaken the alcohol's sting.

"My asshole is relatively regular sized," I said.

We laughed as the afternoon Kraft shift filtered out of the bar, our voices fading into discussions of the weather, the Kansas City Chiefs, workers' comp, and shift differentials. Another firm look from him made my cheeks light on fire, and I got up to order another drink at the bar, an ambivalence hanging somewhere between guilt and excitement.

My boyfriend had moved away to Boston for a PhD program four months before. Paul and I had decided to stay together, get married when he finished. But between Skype calls and text messages, my emotional distance had grown with the physical.

When I came back with a full glass, he was checking baseball scores.

"Who's your team?" I asked, excited to talk about my own favorite sport after spending four years talking about soccer with Paul.

"The Cardinals," he said. "I'm loyal to my Missouri teams. My home."

This made me raise my eyebrows. Curious. *I wonder how he feels about kids.* The thought filled me with self-disappointment as I remembered a call from Paul earlier that day, when, before he hung up the phone, he said, "Boston doesn't feel like home. You feel like home."

But I wondered where that left me if one couldn't go home again. Nothing is ever quite the same, really, but Paul wouldn't have understood the sentiment. He had never read Thomas Wolfe, even when I mentioned he may like it after spending two months on the book for my weekly book club with Norm MacDonald. Instead, he would read Descartes to my son, which I found both endearing and maddening. At the time, Beck was seven, but perhaps those intense intellectual types thought this was a good age to start thinking about dualism and modern philosophy.

He had my son explain the ball of wax experiment, how we can understand it melting in the fire through our minds, through our own reasoning.

"See? Beck gets it," he said. But Beck looked bored, stealing a glance in my direction. He yawned and stared at the floor.

"Smart dude," I said. "But I think we should finish the night with *Harry Potter*."

When I went to bed that night, Paul leaned over. He asked, "What do you think about the philosophy of time?"

"I don't know, Paul." His name came out too hard and distant, even with its soft consonants.

Less than six months later, we would hear back from our graduate schools. He went with Boston, the one farthest away. Maybe that's why I would find myself sitting across from the poet who spoke of fish like he spoke of family, who said death seemed scary but didn't entertain Heideggerian ontology when he mentioned his grandfather passing away.

I had just lost my grandmother, and now my own grandfather was sick, so this felt human. It didn't feel forced.

When we left, he told me that this was nice. He didn't go out with friends often.

"Me either," I said, but I shuffled my feet when I walked back to my car.

*

When I saw the poet at my biannual writers' retreat, I told him hello — distant, shy. I had seen him there for several retreats, but the newfound friendship caused a tightness in my lungs every time I ran into him at a table, at a lecture. Even when we drank outside of his hotel room with a group of familiar friends, I was more distant than usual. I looked to the ground when I laughed.

By eleven o'clock on Friday night, the retreat regulars busted out our usual game of Truth or Truth, which usually left newcomers feeling red faced and awkwardly giggling when they found out the various salacious acts that their new writer companions had explored. The poet talked about the time a girl asked him to Saran Wrap her arms to her torso and then fuck her hard.

My eyebrows shot up. "What was that like?" I asked him.

"Squeaky," he said, taking a long drag off his cigarette.

Everyone laughed. He looked less stiff, comfortable. I laughed too, though I caught myself wondering what sex with him would be like Saran Wrap–free. Did he lack eye contact? Did he talk too much? What would he have said, hovering over a girl with her arms bound tight, completely restricted?

As people filtered to bed throughout the evening, the poet and I sat at the table outside my cabin. For the first time since the bar, we were alone. We were, again, looser and more talkative with booze.

Perhaps too much booze.

There wasn't anyone else outside, not that I could tell. The resort feline, Smudge, sat on the porch watching both of our hands as we talked. The poet fiddled with another cigarette. He coughed into his free hand. But he also spoke with his hands as well, free and unwound. His fingers were tan and long, and although he had a thick build, you wouldn't have been able to tell by looking at his hands. The kind of hands to get lost in—the kind of hands that made me self-conscious about my own fingers, chubby and small. At that moment, they were sweaty, and I wiped them on my jeans, hoping he hadn't noticed. I kept my palms flat, fingers curled over the edges of the bench as the night went on, only moving them when Smudge came over for a rub.

When the cat jumped on the table, the poet took his cigarette-free hand and ran his fingers from head to tail several times in a row. I couldn't look away, eyes too intent on moving hands.

At one point, he had moved beside me. I was talking about Paul, how

I had a series of anxiety attacks after he had left, how I didn't know about him choosing a program so far from home. I didn't know how long I had been talking, and when I realized where the conversation had gone, I began to rub my hands on my jeans again.

He noticed. "Are you okay?" he asked.

"I don't know," I said, which was true, and it was also the first time I remembered answering the question honestly.

The poet was quiet, staring at Smudge, who was back on the porch with eyes half closed, perhaps still listening.

Finally, a break in the silence: "Why are you still with him?"

I remembered the first time Paul had met Beck. He asked if he could go to Beck's baseball game before the semester started in August. I said, "Okay," with some hesitancy. After the game, he gave him a high five and introduced himself—"A friend of your mom's," he told him. Beck looked over at me and smiled, his front teeth missing at the age of five. It felt like we could be a unit—an idea that had always been just out of reach.

*

Another bar night two weeks after the retreat: I went home with him to play cards after all of the whiskey.

The fifty-five-gallon tank greeted me first when I walked in the door, shortly after was his dog.

"Leo," he said. "Off." His voice was direct. His voice Saran Wrap.

He had had the fish for three years. "A long time for freshwater fish," he told me.

He stood next to me, leaning down to point at the green cory cat nosing its way through the pebbles.

"That's Saul," he said. "He's nervous. Like a Jew."

The last sentence came out too sharp, and I shifted my weight, my feet uneasy on the shag carpet. I might have said, "Oh."

"Lazarus—the big black one with a red tail—chases Saul around. I should probably get more fish."

In the aquarium glass, I could see our reflection. His head was cocked toward mine as we watched the two fish, the black one now chasing the smaller green cory cat. His hands were on his hips. In my own reflection, my hands sat at my side, my body neutral.

We don't say anything for a while, watching the fish swim back and forth, never at rest.

Matted and Mangled

Your hair becomes knotted when your brain leans into your sadness, and by the end of the year, you're so matted, your cheeks become saturated in tears whenever you gather enough courage to attempt to brush out the tangles. At this point in your relationship, you'll have expected infidelity but lack any proof, so instead you will cry more and your hair will become more matted, and so on. But he'll throw curveballs, like when he treats you with a soft kindness you haven't seen in years, asking you to lay your head on his lap as he sprays detangler on your wild mane, working in small sections from the bottom up with such care, with such a gentle hand, you feel like maybe the changes in his behavior, the way he looked at you with contempt, was all in your head, just like he always said it was. In six months, you'll stumble onto the affair. Close friends will tell you about the second apartment he somehow paid for with his meager teaching stipend—they'll look you straight in the eye, just like they always had. Like your mother, you'll come to understand how some people choose to stay, and some people go. Unlike your mother, you don't have a window to look out of. But for now, you're in his lap, a wave of unknown safety washing over you that you never want to shake, to let go of, as he cradles your head with one hand and untangles knots with the other. You convince yourself that this scene creates your own kind of private entanglement, a pair that will always be connected, despite the amount of distance between the two. When some knots prove to be too tight, you step outside for a break and stand by each other in silence. He lights a cigarette, says, *I drove by a kitten on the side of the road on my way home. Hit but still alive.* You look over at him—face half-shadowed, stoic—and watch his hands as he details the cat's run-over legs. *I got out of my truck to see if he was worth saving.* When you'll look back to this moment, you'll wonder which home he was headed to. You can still see him acting out the limp limbs with his hands as he smoked a Marlboro 27. You remember the way he breathed out the smoke and told you how he held the kitten in his palms, saying a prayer before breaking its neck, and you remember a gnawing ache in the pit of your gut as you listened, how, even then, you knew he would have never given you the same grace as he did that broken, mangled tabby.

Life Is Too Short Not to Get Beef Jerky from a Van on the Side of a Highway

When we pass the van selling beef jerky on the side of the highway, I say, "We should probably turn back."

Liv laughs. They turn back to look at me to say: "We might get murdered, but it may be worth it." They laugh again.

Sierra, the driver, says, "Maybe next time we come back."

The three of us smell like last night's cranberry wine, eyes baggy from staying up too late, saying goodbye to old friends from the writers' retreat we go to twice a year in southeastern Missouri. Most of them, we only see twice a year.

It's the first weekend in May, and the Ozarks' trees look renewed, revitalized. Even the dogwoods that make the world smell like dog piss have me feeling stirred. I don't mention this to Liv and Sierra despite how they understand I've had a long winter—they'd recognize my need for a fresh lens on growth. But I'd hate to be that turd who entertains transformation clichés, so I stay quiet.

I never get the chance, anyway. Two miles after the van selling beef jerky on the side of the highway, another car merges into our lane. Sierra swerves, and she swerves again to miss a car in another lane. She gasps. She says she's lost control.

A final image: my hands, nearly opaque, trying to hold on to anything solid, and then there are Liv's hands reaching for the grab handle, and Sierra raises her own hands above the steering wheel. A surrender. I say, "Sierra. Your hands. What are you doing with your hands?" unaware that when the tires lose traction, you have to give up. You need to let go completely.

The burgeoning world is hushed, too quiet. I think: *Of course I'm going to die hungover on the way home from a writers' retreat, cranberry wine still seeping out of my pores.* Boozy writers — another cliché.

What's not cliché is the fact that my life didn't flash before my eyes. Only a few images, quick flashes of last memories shared.

*

I think of Beck first, how the two of us lay on our stomachs, elbows propped up, while he rested his hands on his cheeks and the last book I read from rested in my hands. *Harry Potter and the Order of the Phoenix*, a nightly chapter read aloud. The night before I left for the writers' retreat, he ran his fingers through my hair as I read, braiding the left side. He said, "Don't move. Keep it like this forever." He asked for just one more page, but I was too tired for just one more.

When I tucked Beck in that night, he reached his arms out for a ritual hug, his fingers too long for eleven years old. His hands, which have always looked like my hands, even as a baby. "Those are your hands. He has your hands," my mother told me that very first day, when he was scared and I was scared, our similar hands unsure of what to do with this world we had just entered.

Now his hands are just as big. Beck makes it a point to show me how his fingers keep growing longer and thinner, and if it weren't for my chipped fingernails and writing calluses, the scar in the shape of an olive branch dove on my right ring finger, it would be hard to tell whose hands were whose. I watched his hands when he typed a short story on his school laptop. For weeks, I watched him work on the same short story. One time, he caught my gaze. "What?" he asked, and I told him nothing. He told me he wanted to be a writer, and the torn space in between endearing-because-I'm-a-writer and please-don't-turn-out-sad-like-me was so intense and loud that I had to excuse myself to the bathroom. Later, I welled up again when I read a fraction of what he wrote:

Just because I'm different doesn't mean I don't have an education. You may think I'm like seven years ahead while I'm telling this story, but I'm not. This is the night my mom died. Right now she's in front of me, as a ghost. I can summon the dead whenever I want (I learned tonight) but I shouldn't do it too often or else a black hole might open (how do I know this, I don't know. I guess it came to my brain when I was crying on the bathroom floor).

I laughed about the mother being dead. "I hope you weren't thinking about me," I said. Beck said, "No, no. It's just a story, Mom." I told him I liked his use of parentheses, how some college-age students sometimes don't even use them correctly in classes I've taken, classes I've taught. "Yeah, right," he said, embarrassed. "I should just start over." I wished I would have told him how I liked the way "crying on the bathroom floor" sounded, but now, all I can see is him crying on the bathroom floor when he finds out his nonfictional mother is gone. And as the car tires screech past two Amish men on a buggy, I wonder if my son will ever finish *The Order of the Phoenix*. And if so, will I die a second time as Sirius fades behind the Veil, Harry reaching, hands stretched far?

I imagine Beck hearing my voice as he reads, his hands nearly like my hands under the weight of the pages.

*

Beck and I sing Tom Waits ballads in the car. We sing low and raspy. He always says, "What is Tom waiting on, anyway?" Yesterday was the last time I sang out loud, but it wasn't Tom Waits. I was still at the writers' retreat when the rain had blown into the covered porch, a small group sat in a circle underneath, drinking Chris's cranberry wine and talking about that afternoon's panel. I couldn't pay attention to the conversation, not because I wasn't there, but because Neil Diamond's "Sweet Caroline" was playing in my head, only the chorus was replaced with "Cranberry Wine."

Though I had been uncharacteristically withdrawn this writers' retreat, I thought this was important enough to mention to the group, and in a synchronized moment, everyone started to sway and sing together. In Styrofoam cups, the sweet red swished along to the beat as we all pounded *duh, duh, duh.*

Across from me, Sierra smiled, and I knew what the smile meant: You're doing all right, Mama Bird—a nickname she's used since I snuck her alcohol her first retreat three years ago and then made her talk about her life.

Sierra was also there the last time I sang out loud two months ago. March 2—my birthday.

My boyfriend played my favorite song on the bar stereo. I recognized it immediately—the first note in Jeff Buckley's cover of "Hallelujah." I ran over and gave him a kiss on the cheek, sang the verses as we played pool. I joked about not having enough air for that second-to-last hallelujah in the song, the one that goes on forever.

The same night I found out about the affair. Up until "Cranberry Wine," I would only sing in the car by myself. Not because I had a bad voice. I just knew it was never enough. I grew irritated with Buckley every time "Hallelujah" came on, which was seemingly everywhere: a pho shop, a friend's car stereo, a dressing room stall while trying on smaller pant sizes from not being able to stomach anything. When he got to the penultimate *hallelujah*, I wondered if Buckley only held on to the note for so long because he knew he could get away with it.

*

And he was the last person I had sex with, too. Which is such a neat thing to realize when you're about to die.

It was March 5 when I went to his apartment—a place he had kept secret, paying rent for two different places while he pretended the house we shared was a home. I was drunk and trying to hold on to something, anything. He was too rough, grabbing my hair hard and without apology.

I asked him to stop. He grabbed harder, and he didn't let go until I told him it hurt too much. Once he finished, I requested: kiss me like you love me. Afterward, I crept out of his apartment as he snored in the dark.

The last person I kissed was a month later—a fireman I had met via Tinder. Because I didn't want the last person I kissed to be that last person I had sex with. Outside of a closing bar, the fireman tucked a loose hair behind my ear. "You're beautiful," he said, and I acted like I didn't hear him, kissing back with more urgency.

*

Sierra held me two weeks earlier. She was the last person to hold me. I finally went back to the house I had avoided because I found him everywhere—his Cardinals jersey, that fucking mirror in the shape of a guitar, an early copy of *Breakfast of Champions* he gave me three years earlier because I told him it was my teenage favorite. He hid in corners too: guitar picks underneath couch cushions, poetry books mixed into my own bookshelves. He had stopped playing guitar the year before, around the same time he stopped sharing his poetry.

In a moment of unhinged loneliness, I called Sierra. "I'm on my way," she said once she heard my staccato speech. She walked through the front door to find a guitar mirror being smashed. The glass crunched under my feet as I moved onto the beloved book, page by page floating to the floor, and when the only thing left of it was a bare spine, I crumpled onto the couch, holding my shoulders because I didn't know what to do with my hands. Like the tires, I had lost traction completely, but no one ever told me what to do with those hands.

Without a word, Sierra walked over and sat beside me. She wrapped her arms around my whole torso, and she held me as if I were a child. She held me as if I were a baby bird.

*

And even with all that dog shit pain, I told myself it's okay. Because it's spring now, and, in a small moment, I relearned how to sing. I'm able to laugh loosely and probably too loud, like when Timmy cooked his usual midnight barbecue the night before, and John came to round everyone up. "It's time for Timmy's Meat World!" We laughed forever.

Everything I held in the past few months spilled out of my mouth as laughter. For a second, I was certain it would go on forever. Laughter as freeing, and laughter as my own unbroken hallelujah. So, I know there's laughter, and I know there's still a lot of love—love for these people and a green spring. The last person I said "I love you" to wasn't my ex but Beck, while dropping him off at his father's house for the weekend.

We had one of our "quaint dates," as he calls them, which consist of sushi and a small hike on the outskirts of town. Every date, he would ask to try a different kind of nigiri. This week it was eel. "My new favorite," Beck told me with a small smile.

I was late dropping him off because we ventured too far from the path during the hike. We had taken too many forks in the trail and the maples started blurring together as one featureless tree. When he noticed the anxiety, the tightness of my posture and how quick I spoke, Beck said, "We're not dead, Mom. We're just lost."

"Love you, love you, love you," I told him as he closed the door. I said it three times, like my grandmother always did, like I did every time I left the city.

"I'll see you when you get back," he said with that same small smile. This has been the clearest image of all.

*

As I go through this list of lasts, Sierra and Liv sway with the movement of the car, bobbleheads jerking from the highway's rumble strips. My eyes blink hard, or maybe I closed them for too long as the car drives off the road and into the ravine, Sierra's hands still in surrender.

I wait for the vehicle to flip, only to find the wheels have turned and we're now traveling backward. The smell of burnt rubber fades as we come to a stop. Everything is silent, save the tires of the cars driving by. Save our hearts beating too loud as we all fill our lungs with new air after letting out a unified held breath. I can only see the back of Sierra's head, angled down, hands now on the wheel. For the first time this year, I know what to do with my own hands, placing each hand on her shoulders. "We're alive," my words and my hands say.

Two men in an SUV pull over, ask what they can do. We learn they're EMTs off duty. They roll Sierra's car—undamaged, untouched—to the shoulder. One says, "You girls be thankful for the rain this weekend. If the soil had been hard, those tires wouldn't have stayed on the ground."

*

Another cliché: three women nearly die on their way home from a writers' retreat, so they take turns reflecting on how life is too short. They all find out that life seems to be too short for everything, but, in this moment, for one of the women, for certain, life is too short for these things:

Life is too short to not sing songs about cranberry wine with friends while the rain blows around them for the trees and for the ground and for herself. She knows life is too short to not partake in Timmy's Meat World at midnight, and it's too short to feel like she can't laugh freely. Life is too short to not read an extra page to her son at night, to not have "quaint dates," and life is also too short to not have adventures, to not take unexpected turns on a hiking trail, to not get lost just to find your way again. Life is too short to not get beef jerky from a van on the side of a highway.

A big one: Life is too short to be afraid to start over new. Life is too short to have to ask someone to kiss her like they loved her. Too short to notice how her partner no longer calls her beautiful. Too short for lukewarm love, love half-filled. Not really love at all, she'll tell herself, just a vacant emotion that builds under dirty fingernails and instead of washing his hands completely, he'll scrape the crud out of the visible edges and say, "That'll do." The woman knows life is too short for that'll do.

*

Future: Sierra will fall to her knees onto her living room floor, fingers spread wide across the carpet. She'll take a long breath, hold it in. Her mouth will nearly kiss the fibers. She'll say, "I love how the ground feels." She'll repeat it again: "I love how the ground feels: so solid, so safe."

When I leave, she'll hug me. She'll breathe in my hair. She'll say, "Love you, Mama Bird." I'll hug her back. I'll hold her a little bit longer this time.

When I remove my arms, I'll think of the last person I hugged before her, earlier that morning. John was leaving the retreat to go back home to St. Louis, where his wife and two cats were. At the time, I didn't know how, hours later, I'd be thinking about this last memory after nearly dying by a van of beef jerky. I didn't know I'd be asking what ifs, like what if it hadn't rained, Sierra's car rolling, Liv crushed as the car turned to its side? What if Sierra hadn't swerved to avoid the car at all, and next retreat, there'd be three empty seats, Chris pouring out some cranberry wine while someone reads in memory of? What if Sierra hadn't raised her hands in the air—what if she hadn't let go?

Earlier that morning, John had sighed as he looked at the trees and the Ozarks' hills, the river louder as the rain softened. He looked over at me and said, "I love this place," and I wasn't sure if it was meant for me or for him or for us or for the place itself, so I just sighed and looked out, too. He continued, "I love this place because I know, without a doubt, that if I ever died, people would remember me here. I love this place because it is a home, and it's your home, too, even after everything he did."

*

When I finally get back to my empty bedroom, I will think of the word *home*. I will swish it around in my mouth, hands raised in the air.

Dissonance

When you find yourself in the car listening to Jeff Buckley's "Hallelujah," you think back to the previous year. It was an especially cold October, and a pair of mice had found refuge in your hundred-year-old home. You were playing rummy with your boyfriend, sipping on a forty of Olde English as the two mice snuck between half-empty cereal boxes. When you lost a game, you looked up to find one of them staring at you, whiskers twitching, daring you to try and catch him. Or her. You're convinced it's a romantic duo, the way they squabbled back and forth, and with your luck, the house would contain a thriving rodent family by early November.

Despite the impending mouse doom, you found yourself smiling as the chords of "Hallelujah" crept up through the speaker. Forty seconds into the song is your favorite moment—when Buckley was so moved by the pairing of chords that he moaned along with his guitar, as if moved his Telecaster could make such a noise.

You looked away from the mouse. You said, "That moan. I love how Jeff can still be surprised by music."

"Yeah," your boyfriend said back, unfazed, looking down at a fresh hand of cards. Maybe it was then that you understood the first verse of the song. The song as a whole, actually. Perhaps this was why you were unsurprised by your last conversation, when you asked if he was even sorry, and he said *not at all*. The house remained empty besides you, your son who you had half the week, and a nuclear family of mice neither you or your boyfriend had ever bothered to catch.

*

Your life is marked by several odd notes coming together, sometimes all at once, the sound ringing in your ears for days at a time. The collision has its own beauty. And one of the most striking noises you've struggled through was having your son, who is now eleven and impatient and inquisitive and too smart and kind.

This is normal. I'm doing well. It's a mantra you repeat often, ever since you gave birth at seventeen. You'd like to think you say it less and less each year, but you don't. You'll say it under your breath while the two of you share a sushi dinner as you tell him the difference between nigiri and sashimi (*I'm doing well*, as you watch him dip the yellowtail roll into soy sauce and smile when he closes his eyes, breathes in, content and warm). A couple sits beside you, and the wife catches your eye, gives you an awkward smile that you read as: How young is she, anyway? And you'll tell yourself *This is normal. I'm doing well.*

Before your son falls asleep tonight, the two of you talk in his twin bed, heads sharing the same pillow as you look up at plastic stars. When he was eight, you tried to arrange them in constellation patterns, but stopped at the Big Dipper and Orion when you realized you didn't have enough of them and couldn't afford to buy more. *I'm doing well*, you told yourself. And in any case, you had forgotten the shape of Cygnus, of Sirius and Pisces.

It had been four years since you took a course in astronomy, but you'll find the loss of knowledge especially bothersome, as if poor memory reflects parental worth. So you talk about the details you can remember.

"Hey, Beck." You say his name in a whisper, as if what you're about to say is a secret only the two of you will share.

"Yeah?"

You pause, trying to remember the important cosmological facts, but only a few things come to mind.

"Did you know that there is another side of the moon we never see? It's called the far side of the moon." *Or is it the dark side?* you wonder, always second guessing.

"Why can't we see it?" he asks.

"It's locked with earth as it orbits," you say, hoping he doesn't press you on why or how this is the case.

"How do we know what the other side looks like?"

"Science," you joke, and he laughs with you.

You want to keep up the moment. *I'm doing well.* You tell him about Dragonfly 44, the Milky Way's dark twin that you read about last week. How it's made of mostly dark matter, unlike other galaxies held together by the attraction of stars.

"Is dark matter bad?" he asks.

"Yes. We're all going to die. Probably very soon." You feel his head shift as he looks over at you. You look back, and he rolls his eyes with a smile. "No," you say. "It's not bad. It's just something we don't understand. That's why Dragonfly 44 is important. Before, we hardly knew anything about dark matter. Now we know it can hold whole galaxies together."

When you think of dark matter, you will think of your ex, finishing his forty as the mice run through a maze of unfinished groceries. You think of discordant keys coming together and the way that ex said, "I love you," that night—distant, manufactured—almost as if he meant to say, "I loved you," instead.

Beck doesn't notice the lull in the conversation. He doesn't say anything either. You can tell he's thinking, it's the same intent gaze he has after finishing a novel. On a drive three months after the breakup, you asked your son why he was so serious after he closed the last book of the Percy Jackson series.

"I just didn't want it to end. I wanted to know what happens after, what everyone is up to," he explained.

You empathized. You also easily get attached to characters and ideas and books and words. But, instead, you told him, "It's okay. It ends where it ends because everything turned out where it needed to be, and you learned the story the author wanted to tell. Besides, everything will be boring afterward. They'll all just be doing day-to-day things. You know everything you need to know."

Unlike the endings of books, dark matter will likely remain a mystery. And this bothers Beck, who asks, "But. But what else does it mean? When will we learn more?"

You say, more to yourself than to him: "We can't know everything." You kiss him goodnight, wish him sweet dreams.

*

In music theory, you learn the importance of dissonant sounds in a musical piece. Some theorists argue an entire composition of consonant sounds may become mundane for the audience. Dissonance, in contrast, builds of tension, offering a more purposeful resolution when the movement between unstable chords and those final, harmonious notes.

The existential dissonance is a necessity. Unstable moments of time allow for a more meaningful orchestrated existence, and when all the seemingly disjointed things come together, they move toward a purposeful, singular beauty. Like dark matter, discordancy isn't inherently bad—it's something we attempt to understand despite an overwhelming uncertainty, the unanticipated end grand in its own distinction.

In the morning you'll drop your son off at school. On the back road in between is where you'll hear Jeff Buckley's moan again, and although the song brings you back to last year's card game, you only entertain the memory for a moment. After all, despite the jarring heartbreak, your life didn't stay emotionally muddled forever. Your son no longer asks about your ex, and, eventually, you caught all the mice alive, drove them down the block, and put them in the trees at the edge of the neighborhood. You move on when you decide it was for the best, that whoever comes into your lives next will be someone who doesn't love in past tense, a person your son would someday want to be. And for now, you're learning how to be okay with being alone, occasionally reminding yourself: *This is normal. You are doing well.*

If You Build It, Baseball Dads Will Come

When you left, Baseball Dads started to pop up everywhere: the man in the Royals hat at Arts Fest looking at green-glazed ceramics, or the car mechanic who changes my oil and fixed my calipers last June. A Baseball Dad could be any man at the grocery store carrying the right build. Dad-ish. Fit-ish. Baseball-ish. There was the running joke between me and my friend, Shane, about the Baseball Dad who coached the fourth-grade team Beck was on. Before practice, I'd throw the ball with Beck, and when Baseball Dad got there, he'd say, "Great arm," or "Nice one," or "Looking good." The first time this happened, I sighed when he walked away, squinting my eyes to see if he had a wedding ring. For an instant, I thought he was talking to me.

I messaged Shane after the first practice. "I think I'm in love with Beck's coach."

"What's he like? Does he have nice arms?" Shane asked.

"A-plus arms. He wears Ray-Bans when it's sunny out and has a nice smile." I paused, adding, "That's enough for me right now."

Enough for me was anything that kept me from getting too quiet, too serious—whether it was fantasizing about another life with Baseball Dad (or anyone who was kind to me, really) or porch nights with Shane, where we laughed at Tinder profile pictures featuring men holding a big ass trout or bass.

Sometimes, Shane would just listen to me cry.

Beck recognized the moments I got too quiet, too. Perhaps the giveaway was the shape my face took when a memory resurfaced. Or maybe my son could hear my heartbeat increase or the way I forgot to breathe when overcome with that quiet.

Beck would just smile. He would say, "Breathe," and I would breathe.

*

We listened to Mike Shannon on Cardinals Radio for three seasons: his voice filling the corners of silence on early summer drives when approaching dusk lit up with fireflies, his voice pouring over crackling vegetables in the skillet that you'd toss in the air from time to time, showing off techniques you learned from the Mexican restaurant you worked at while juggling graduate school and teaching. You thought it was cool how, in 1996, I saw Ozzie Smith's last game, and I liked that you loved the Cardinals because you were the kind of man to root for home.

You repeated these Shannonisms, the endearing things Mike said during home games and, if we were lucky, an away game just close enough for him to travel. I can't remember them now—the Shannonisms—but there's an appropriately-named website that will give you a new Shannonism every time you refresh the screen via clicking on a dancing image of Mike Shannon, smiling wide with all his teeth.

What I do remember: The first time you played catch with Beck. I cooked dinner while the two of you stood in the backyard. From the open kitchen window, I caught myself smiling when I heard you give him pointers: line up with the target, use your entire body.

Beck asked me when you would be coming back for another round—if I could join, too. During the warm months, we'd form a triangle, the ball going back and forth, dogs watching from the sliding door.

We started watching Cardinals games at sports bars with Beck. You would drink your whiskey and Coke, eyes up at the screen. During commercial breaks, you'd leave to smoke a cigarette outside, and I'd see you looking through your phone, taking a long drag with your head down. And although it bothered me you couldn't wait to smoke whenever we left, I'd forget the irritation soon after you came back and patiently explained the game to Beck when he asked questions.

Like: "What's an RBI?"

"An RBI stands for Runs Batted In," you told Beck, who listened hard, eyes focused. You pointed at the recap playing on the television and continued, "Whenever a batter hits a ball and someone makes it home, the batter will get an RBI. See, look: Matt Holliday hit the ball down the left and got onto second. But he also got Carpenter to the home plate—a Run Batted In." Everything you said sounded like home.

*

The next summer, I watched fireflies from Shane's porch. We'd talk about how the Cardinals and Cubs were neck and neck for first in the NL Central.

"You know, my dad likes baseball."

"I should fuck your dad," I joked and immediately felt bad. "I don't think I could do that to your mom," I added.

"I know, buddy. I know."

*

I thought of Mike Shannon when I found out about your second life—your second apartment, your second girlfriend who thought you were going to propose after only a third of the amount of time you and I had been together. I found out a month before opening day on my birthday. I thought of Mike Shannon's voice filling the corners of a more unsettling silence. Not the kind of quiet speckled with firefly lights or vegetables cooking, but the kind where my son reminded me to breathe. So I never turned the radio back on, replacing his voice with television games at a sports bar we never went to. I graded or read or thought about maybe writing again, and I'd watch any game offered on the screen. I even kept track of the Cubs whenever Jason Heyward was traded from the Cards, a new interest offering both a Baseball Crush as well as the satisfaction that you weren't happy about the stats that season. You weren't the type of baseball fan who loved the beauty of the game, but instead, reveled hard in rivalry—sometimes even direct hatred—all masked underneath being the kind of man who always rooted for home.

I began to pack away our own home, and if it got too quiet, I would go down to the sports bar just to silently be with others. Sometimes these others were Men-Who-Explain-Baseball-To-Me—men who tried to talk to me while I went back and forth between watching a game and grading. This wasn't new. When I first transition from Shannon to television, some male bartenders asked if I *actually* liked baseball—eyebrows raised as they wiped the counter. One patron deconstructed baseball on an atomic level. I gave him a tight smile, cut him short when he got to RBIS. "That's enough for now, guy," and I'd get back to my work. I learned that I loved frowning vacantly at douchebags.

Through a stream of baseball games and public solitude via grading at sports bars, I also learned I could find comfort in being alone.

As October approached and Tinder dates passed, Mansplaining Baseball became a norm. But so did rolling my eyes or being okay with silence. I watched every game of the Cubs playing the Indians, and fuck, did you miss a beautiful chorus of drunk bros and a drunk me with drunk friends singing, "Go! Cubs! Go!" when they finally won. I didn't think too much of you. For an instant, I wondered if that machismo-enriched-rivalry had clouded appreciating the sportsmanship of both the Indians and the Cubs in the most remarkable World Series in our lifetimes. I hoped it didn't, and I kept singing. Like Mike Shannon taught me, "Don't bite your head off to spite your nose."

*

The only regret I have is realizing too late that he wasn't essential enough to be the *you* in this narrative. But a new season is with us now. I can feel the approaching flock of Men-Who-Explain-Baseball-to-me, but I also foresee tossing the ball with Beck, perhaps playing keep-away with my new partner in the middle, someone who doesn't know much about baseball at all.

Step Five

How to Mourn a Nation

In Missouri, hand-painted billboards reading TRUMP are scattered along the highway, and even more Trump signs litter neighborhood streets and business windows. People kept them up after the election, and even before his time was done, they had billboards and posters and signs and bumper stickers for 2016 and 2020 and 2024 and some that demanded his ruling forever. His campaign birthed minions within Missouri politics, like Eric Greitens, who ran for governor with an ad of him shooting machine gun rounds as a narrator knights him as a "conservative warrior," who fights back by "bringing out the big guns." He was elected, though he resigned only a year and a half in because of sexual misconduct and violations of campaign finance law—just enough time to gut funding for social services, higher education, and the arts. Missouri also has Josh Hawley, the most unapologetic cuck in the Senate.

In 2016, you become hyperaware of how you navigate the world as a woman. You watch the largest single-day protest for women, and a part of you feels galvanized from the energy. By 2021, your state will be the first to illegalize abortion. Your attorney general rushed to sign a proclamation minutes after the Supreme Court overturned *Roe*, even tweeting: "This is a monumental day for the sanctity of life." A week later, a woman almost died in St. Louis because of pregnancy complications at three in the morning. The legal team wasn't available to confirm whether or not doctors could give her the care she needed.

You've hardly recovered from Trump's first campaign. The day after he was elected, you woke up on your friend's couch—eyes puffy, mascara streaked—and immediately cried into a pillow. Your friend's beagle consoled you between sobs. When Hillary's concession speech was made and things were truly solidified, you took tequila shots at eleven in the morning with an indie bookstore owner you ended up kissing in the pub, because what else could go wrong?

You're not sure how to properly mourn a nation, and everyone is telling you to keep moving, not to give up, but here you are almost a decade later, older and waning.

Mein(e) C—

15.

The plastic speculum I stole from the doctor's office when I was twenty sat in the back seat of my car for a year, serving as a vaginal conversation piece for friends, family, acquaintances, and men who may have wanted to be the speculum itself. They'd ask why I had the speculum. They'd ask where I got the speculum. Sometimes, the men would ask, "What is a speculum?" Sometimes the women asked, too.

"A speculum is a friend of the female family," I'd tell them with a smile. More than once, I'd be kind enough to contextualize further, holding the speculum in hand while puppeteering the clamps up and down. A master ventriloquist as the words fell out of my mouth.

Together, the speculum and I would say to both the men and the women, "I taste vaginal walls to see if they are sad, if there's anything wrong. Speculums exist because no one wants a mopey vagina."

Female friends would laugh, some with red faces (SO UNCOUTH, THAT GIRL).

Men would pause, perhaps thinking, *Wait, I don't have fucking vaginal walls.*

14.

A. Oxford English Dictionary

   1. Cunt /kʌnt/

   a. [Probably the reflex of an Old English form *cunt* that is not securely attested (cognate with Old Frisian *kunte*), Middle Dutch *conte* (Dutch *kont*), Middle Low German *kunte*, Middle High German *kunt*, Old Icelandic *kunta* (only as a byname), Norwegian *kunte*, Swedish regional *kunta*, *kutta*, Danish *kunte*, further etymology uncertain].

13.*a*.

A. Urban Dictionary

User, "Asscaver," defines a speculum as an anal or vaginal pry bar.

a. Example: "The doctor put his speculum in my wife's cooch, so I told him to throw an extra stitch or 2 in there for me when he was done." Asscaver receives nineteen thumbs up, nine thumbs down. In support of America's erogenous Capitalism, you can purchase a mug sporting the definition for only twenty-five dollars + tax.

13.*b*.

A. Oxford English Dictionary

Speculum, /ˈspɛkjʊləm/, [< Latin *speculum*, < *specĕre* to look (at), observe]

12.

Helene Cixous explains White Ink, or *écriture féminine*, as a counter to phallogocentricism—what Derrida coined as male-privileged writing, explaining how language was constructed by men and for men with a phallic agenda. In consequence, phallogocentricism marginalized women within the confines of her only means of oral or written communication. Phallocentric ideology inhibits semiotics to the male experience, leaving women without a signified to convey her own story. Cixous says that to embrace White Ink, women must explore her own body and identity; she must write with her body, and in writing with and through and for her body, she will find her voice. She will find her song.

Lost through centuries of subjugation, "speculum," a word embodying scientific objectivity ("to look at, to observe"), can be dwindled down into a *vaginal pry bar*. There is loaded language even in Urban Dictionary: *his speculum, my wife's cooch* (And while you're in their doc, could you patch her up so I can feel better during what is, without a doubt, some one-sided banging? Kthanks).

11.

Clarice Lispector, *Água Viva*

"What am I in this instant?
>I am a typewriter making the dry keys echo in the dark and humid early hours. For a long time
>I haven't been people.
>>They wanted me
>>to be, an
>>object.

I'm an object. An object dirty with blood."

10.

A. Oxford English Dictionary

1. C—, cont'd

a. History of Usage:

—formerly quaint

—"Despite widespread use over a long period cunt remains the English word most avoided as taboo. It is normally considered the strongest swear word, frequently written with asterisks or dashes to represent suppressed letters, so as to avoid the charge of obscenity."

9.

Days after Trump's pussy-grabbing video surfaced, a woman was confronted in a local sandwich shop in Chicago by a man who told her, "Once Trump is elected, I can grab your pussy all I want." Spencer's Gift's began selling "Grab America by the Pussy" shirts. And shortly after his inauguration, a girl in fourth grade was groped by her fellow classmate without question, without a pause. The boy's logic? If the president can do it, so can I.

8.

The genitives his, whose, and yours (plural) existed in Middle English.
There was no genitive possessive for women.

7.a.

A. Urban Dictionary

1. Pussy, /po͞osē/

a. Man's favorite toy; a man's staple diet; one of the two main food groups; man's best food; dessert; the delicious hot pocket of life; God's gift to men; something God gave to women so men would talk to them; a dick's gate to heaven; the recreational drug quickly becoming the downfall of the male gender; what a female has to bring a man happiness; generally, the only reason to talk to women.

Other acceptable reasons: "Yo, fetch me a beer," or "Blow me." But pussy is also where a man retires after a long hard day; one of the only *things* a man needs from a woman, alongside: cooking, cleaning, and a stress reliever to beat the shit out of. Pussy is: some*thing* that rides your dick, gets torn up; pussy is something men enjoy eating and destroying; pussy is a soft warm spot where your dick can be placed. Pussy is always ready for a good fuck — something to cum inside of; a special place to shove love milk; a box I came in. And another thing pussy is the *thing* that has a woman attached to it. Pussy is: a glove, a mitten, a mitten for a dick, and pussy is a hole the cock goes into, a hole between the legs of some bitch; a hole; that black magic hold for men. Pussy is: a man cave, a meat wallet, a bearded clam, a cum dumpster, squish mitten; ham locker, a box, a box, a box; pussy is a c —-.

b. A pussy is some*thing* to grab.

6.

Clarice Lispector, *Água Viva*:::::

It demands.
The mechanism demands and demands my life.
But I don't
   obey totally: if I must be an object
       let it be an object that screams.

There's a thing inside me that hurts.
Ah how it hurts and how
   itscreamsforhelp.

5.

The morning of November 9, I left black mascara stains on a friend's couch pillow. Her beagle tried to console me through Hillary's concession speech. The day before, I went to cast my vote for the first female presidential nominee of a major party. My mother stood just to my right as we voted, separate but together. My mother taught me it's okay to be strongly woman in a male-dominated world, reaffirming not to be apologetic about that strength. It's okay to be heard.

We cast our ballots at a small Baptist church in the corner of Missouri's Ozark Mountains. It's the same church we attended after my parent's divorce, where I read salacious parts of the Bible during sermons, my brother and I laughing at Song of Solomon 7:8 in the back pews — *I said, I will go up to the palm tree, I will take hold of the boughs thereof: now also thy breasts shall be as clusters of the vine, and the smell of thy nose like apples.* It's the same church where I practiced Bible Drill every Wednesday and eventually got three-years State Perfect, which made for weird trauma but a good detail to tell people at parties. I could puppeteer Leviticus 19:18 with a plastic speculum, mouthing, "You shall love your neighbor as yourself: I am the Lord," but you'd have to listen to me laugh at the absurdity of that addendum, as well as hear a tangent about how the flavor of Christianity in the Ozarks actively forgets this verse when it could help their neighbors most.

In 2005, the pastor told me to write a letter to the congregation, which acted more as an apology for getting pregnant at seventeen and having sex out-of-wedlock. In the letter, I asked for forgiveness and care. I asked for love. The pastor edited the letter to make my case a case for sin. He didn't ask for my son's father to write an apology, despite him being three years older than me and a member of the same congregation.

After the 2016 election, the church had another scandal between the new (and married) music minister and an eighteen-year-old girl. When that same pastor found out, the matter was swept under the rug—without a letter, without the sin being used as ammunition to proselytize.

The music minister went on a leave of absence with pay.

This place could make me angry, but what I remember more than my dislike of the pastor is how my church family rallied in my support. They threw me a baby shower despite the pregnancy being taboo. There's a picture tucked away in one of my mother's storage boxes that I've avoid returning to: I'm not showing yet, but I'm smiling. Behind me is a baby stroller I could never afford. I had clothes and diapers and bibs and handmade blankets and more hope than I had possessed the day before. The people in that congregation were my angels, and I loved them all, even if I no longer understood Christianity.

4.

A. Oxford English Dictionary

1. C—-, n. (*coarse slang*)

a. The female genitals; the vulva or vagina.

o 1680 EARL OF ROCHESTER et al. *Poems* 77

"I fear you have with interest repaid, Those eager

Thrusts, which at your Cunt he made."

o 1956 S. BECKETT *Malone Dies* 24

"His young wife had abandoned all hope of bringing

him to heel, by means of her cunt, that

trump card of young wives."

o 1990 'EURUDICE' F/32 31

"The first penetration brings my death;

I can't see, hear, think: I am all cunt."

3.

Clarice Lispector, *Água Viva*:::::

I'm an object without destiny. I am
an object in whose hands? such is

my human destiny.

What saves me is the scream.
I am an urgent object.

2.

A. Écriture Féminine

    1. Sea of Pink, /si-əv-pɪŋk/, [first-generation etymology]

    a. Phallogocentricsim deconstructed, the white space of the text carried what was unsaid, the margins of history which whispered her untold stories; a dialectic of Her, voices building on one another steadily in polyphony; See Also: *White Ink*

1.

A. Mein(e) C—, or "My (+Germanic feminine possessive) Cunt,"

    1. phrase denoting a reclamation of voice, a unifying scream

    a. not for offense or perversion—more of my own endearing ("ha ha funny", not "ho ho funny") appropriation of an infamous white leader's book title. Mein(e) C—- is to say: a vagina shouldn't be our struggle; it shouldn't be our Mein Kampf.

    It's to say: this body is mine and cannot be brushed up against accidentally or blatantly groped. Our pussies cannot be casually grabbed.

    Mein(e) C—is to say "pussy" and "cunt" is ours, regardless of a lack of possession throughout history.

> CUNT is not:
>
> a thing to be caught by;
>
> the trump card of young wives;
>
> the death of her;

Mein(e) C—is to say: to be heard, movement shouldn't require
a line of three million dressed in pink marching, stretching their arms
across the globe. (But) despite what it shouldn't have taken or
what ought to have been different, there is a growing and powerful

reassurance in knowing what a sea of pink sounds like:
>
> an impenetrable wall of altos and sopranos, but not a wall which
>
>> divides, displaces;
>
>> a unity of voices, songs found in that screaming of magenta and rouge, our cheeks rosy from the cold wind that we refuse to get beneath our skin.

Reclaiming Voices Like Needles in Haystacks

I.

███████'s parents were worried about their daughter kissing other middle school girls. They walked into her room during a sleepover, their daughter's tongue and another's daughter's tongue intertwined. To fix the *issue*, ███████ was taken to see a therapist, who stroked his beard as he listened to ███████ say something like, "I know there is something wrong for me for wanting to kiss them back," or, "I don't want to be different." And the therapist and his beard nodded together as he told her, "It's okay to react back. It's human nature." For a moment, ███████ felt comforted, less isolated. That is, the young teenager felt comforted, less isolated until the therapist walked toward her, until he placed his adult body closer to her own body, his hands reaching without apology.

███████ tells me the story, eyes watching the heart of the fire outside her tent. It's the second and final night of a biannual writer's retreat. Her narrative isn't unprompted, but rather a form of an apology after asking if I was okay, how she had noticed there was a shift in my voice and the way I carried my body since she last saw me.

I told ███████ about the night before, how, at the end of the evening, someone in a position of authority at the ███████ Writer's Retreat saw me walking alone and called me over. He asked where I was sleeping, said he wanted to talk. He mistook my acknowledgment for interest and pressed his face against mine, prying his tongue between closed teeth. My voice got low when I told her how I said into his mouth, "Please stop." And again: "Please just stop," but my words dissipated, and they did again when he wanted more.

Later I would ask if he hadn't heard me. He said he did but kept going. I wasn't prepared for an answer like that, and I could only muster, "You can't do that." But he already knew that, so my words and the moment were swept under one rug or another. A narrative all-too-common—the course of our history is an Everest of amassed rugs hiding swept voices under the heaps.

II.

When ▓▓▓▓▓ tells her story, her words match the tone of the event with the therapist: noncommittal. Avoiding direct disclosure, she'll say, "... and then he felt me up." Her voice gets quieter even though no one could hear her besides me. For a handful of moments, we are silent. The space our voices filled is replaced by the rush of the river and the noise of fire dying.

In the quiet, I think about the way she carefully traversed a memory through disconnected language. I've seen others do this before, how they maneuvered around moments of unwanted attention—voices drifting yet wingless.

Because if the voice of a woman is too quiet, too sensitive, she is insouciant.

Because if a woman's voice is too loud, she is irascible.

I'm slow to realize how I use this noncommittal language, too. Because when I said *unwanted attention*, what I want to say is *invading spaces*, and when I say *invading spaces*, what I really mean is *assaulting our bodies*.

▓▓▓▓▓ says *felt me up*.

Translated: *When my body began burgeoning toward womanhood, a hand I was told to trust assaulted my body, assaulted my potential trust in x, y, and z.*

Or: *His full-grown hands grabbed my young breasts.*

Or: *I don't know how to reclaim my voice, too.*

III.

There are often layers of rugs. When I moved past my silence of being raped at fourteen, I also used indirect language. I wrote because my mother didn't know how to talk about it. The words felt out-of-body, re-watching my teenage self as a grown woman.

The words surfaced—evasive, disconnected. I slanted away from possessive pronouns: *This happened to me.* This is an event. This is not the story fourteen-year-old me or fourteen-year-old ▮▮▮▮ wanted. It's not what thirty-year-old me or thirty-year-old ▮▮▮▮ wanted, either.

These aren't *our* stories.

Because even though the *I* reads as the subject when I say, *This happened to me*, it feels like the *I* acts as the invisible indirect object.

When I wrote about being assaulted at fourteen, I imagined it was more uncomfortable for the reader because of my inclination toward impassivity. Or: I thought it was more uncomfortable for the reader until an essay about my rape was published. The overwhelming accessibility of what happened to me at fourteen forced me to tear down a partition I constructed between myself and the world, as well as the wall I built between myself and self.

IV.

Hélène Cixous, would say a woman can reclaim her body through writing. In writing, women can find our unique female voices, our individual songs. I want to ask her what comes after writing. How do we retrieve parts of us swept away, reclaiming voices like needles in haystacks; or: how to find voice when voice blends in with all the other dust swept under mountains of rugs.

Maybe the needle can be found in small-but-poignant moments of dying fires and soft river waters—a crescendo awakening when two previously-imposed-upon bodies come together in a hushed fellowship.

In recognition, one soul says to another, *I'm sorry this happened to you.*

And the other soul releases a held breath, says the only thing it knows how to say: *I'm sorry, too.* What she means to say: *Thank you for staying with me, for seeing me. I see you, too.*

Twitter's Hot Takes on Women in Politics

Part One

TWITTER EXPLAINS TO MELANIA HER BEING-IN-THE-WORLD

Melania is the queen of   c——;   This woman
is the walking epitome of a thundering c—   which is the
                                        creature of another   stripe;
Melania Trump   is a dumb bitch   c—   who cannot speak
                                                English   correctly.
[She] is a   disgrace to America;
Melania Trump was a birther. She's a   c—;
@FLOTUS   POS C—;
@FLOTUS   c—;
@FLOTUS   Bully   c—;
@FLOTUS   you plagiarist c—;
Melania is   c—;
Melania is   so c—   oh my   god;
Melania is a   c—;
Melania Trump is a   bitch and a c—;
Melania Trump is a   c—. Pass it on;

MELANIA'S-BEING-WITH-THE-WORLD ALSO EXPLAINED IN 140
CHARACTERS OR LESS

Melania Trump you   c—.   Thank God
(your) all over the   news and the truth
                                                    is out..

Melania just proved   #MichelleSaidItBetter;
(she's)   a   oxgen wasting

                                    dumbass plagiarizing
                                            Michelle's speech won't
                                                            save
(her)   from
(being)   the   hollow ass c—
(she)   already is;
           Who the FUCK allows
(that)   c—
@MelaniaTrump to PRAY AT A   @realDonaldTruump
                                        my-dick-is-bigger-rally?
Fuck you both, non-   Christians
        #Impeach45;
Melanie Trump is a   wile wee c—   fukin move to the
                                            White House; Just
            FUCK THAT C—

MELANIA TRUMP;
[her] speech on cyber bullying proves that
[she's]   a dumb c—   who should fucking kill
[herself].

"COMPUTER SCREEN, ARE THERE ACTUALLY BEINGS
INSTEAD OF NOTHINGS?"

                                There's a reason Melania has
    to shove a shower-head up her   c—;   Does   anyone have a
    Picture of Melania Trump's   c—?;
Melania has nice tits. #flotus #bullying #haters #Mel ania #Trump
    #MelaniaTrump #Whore #c—#abuseofpower #unAmericanwhore
    #taxes #lowiq #cumlovinghooker #bitch;
        Let's admire this excellent cow {{Melania photo, after photo}}:
        →would smash
            →somewhat begrudgingly of course
                →Overrated these days...
                    →C—looks like an atrocious ride, tbh
                        →hot c——though

132   TWITTER'S HOT TAKES

{{Melania + Ivanka, smiles tight but focused on camera}}
   →Ivanka's already 35 years old, a total hag.

HEIDEGGERIAN CONSIDERATENESS IN THE DIGITAL WORLD.

{{Photo of Melania on telephone. A meme.

[She]   whispers in large white font: It's Melania again.
                                        You promised if
[I]   give   you leaks
                                            you would bring
[me]   to safe house.   Donald is coming.
[I]   have to go. Please hurry}}.

The meme is pinned on Pinterest — something to remember for laughs at parties. The user writes underneath the photo, a message of consideration at the front of her mind:

"Too bad! [This] c — deserves any misery coming [her] way."

Part Two

THE INTERNET AS AN ONTOLOGICAL RESOURCE FOR MICHELLE

I. Average-Everydayness for Michelle

My 2207 tweet goes to Michelle Obama for being a c — face; I found your keys up in Michelle's Obama's c — . You must have dropped them in there when you were first fucking her; I can't believe that time traveling c — Michelle Obama would steal Melania Trump's speech; The First C — @FLOTUS Michelle Obama says kids should monitor their families for not supporting government; @MichelleObama C —; @MichelleObama is a c —; @MichelleObama you are a real c —; Hey c — @MichelleObama; Yeahhh ur still a c —;

II. Average-Everydayness

@MichelleObama you ruined Chick Fil a Wednesay's you fucking c —; Thanks for the cardboard rice krispy treats you stupid ass c —; Thanks for ruining my lunch you fucking c—@MichelleObama; Hello @MichelleObama get over yourself you self righteous c—; bout to write a HATEFUL letter to Michelle Obama; My mom told me and my sister were to have the same lunch, shed bring us food everyday because @MichelleObama is a c—#gomom; @MichelleObama you stupid fucking c—fuck you for fucking up school lunches you dumb sp**k

III. Average-Everydayness

@MichelleObama Hey, guy, how are you today, c—? Still eating bricks? Ur gay lover still golfing? Can't wait to piss on your grave; @FOXNews @MichelleObama He/she's a c—, they go low we go high; @MichelleObama hey c—. We trust government much more than when ur muslim POS husband was in charge. #MAGA #Trump2020; Slut whore c—is a piece of shit just like her fucking retard husband; @MichelleObama is a lying c—who will say anything to further her agenda ... just like @HillaryClinton; #TRASH;

IV. Average-Everydayness

I sware #michelleobama is sooo c—omg what is that beat face, && c—pearl! YESSSSS J; What's black, hairy and smells of B.O.? Michelle Obama's c—; She's finally got her lifetime title: First C—! What a difference a year makes! God bless the real heritage of FLOTUS (Melania) Now that the Kenyan's wife is gone!; This gorilla C—NEEDS TO BE PUT BACK IN HER CAGE AT THE ZOO WHERE SHE BELONGS; @MichelleObama Racist c—; your portraits ... really. You are a racist c—@MichelleObama; Remember: @MichelleObama is a useless yeast infested c—only fit for hanging{RT HuffPost article, "Michele Obama Embraces her FOREVER First Lady 'Nickname'"} WHAT A DESPICABLE GORILLA C—. THIS BITCH SHOULD BE IN JAIL OR THE ZOO.

Part Three

THE INTERNET AS AN ONTOLOGICAL RESOURCE FOR HILLARY

I. Apophantisch in 140 Characters or Less: Male Lens

Hillary	the killery	c—fromhell;
Hillary	Clinton is a	lyingc—;
Hillar—		ClintonC—t: Adult diaper scrapings

                                                    #BadIceCreamFlavors
    And person who says its all right to have an abortion up until birth is
no Christian And
    that was your   oldc—t
    Hillar—.
    I fucking hate
    Hilla——.
    I hate her entire family;
    Why can't
    Hilla——   understand
                      she lost cause she's a dustyoldc—twho
                                    practiced witchcraft;

    Fuck off
    Hill——   you   toxicoldc-nt;
    Calling
    Hill——   ac-ntisacompliment;
    Because #
    Hil——   Clinton is an evil,nefarious,
                                     andvenalc-nt;

                      [A song]:::::
            Twinkle twinkle little star Hil —— is a c-nt. Hey.

II. Apophantisch in 140 Characters or Less: Female Lens

    Hi—— is a lying cunt;
        Hi—— Cl—— is still a cunt;
                            I feel that   those who voted
    for H——   really only
        wanted   a cunt in office. I don't play the gender card.

II. Being-Toward-Death in a digital age, where nothing and no one can die.

    Fuck H—— C——.   I truly hope she
        drops dead.
        Evil cunt.
        Fuck you——.   Go

TWITTER'S HOT TAKES   135

                die you stupid
fucking   cunt;
——————is a
            cunt,,a massive
            cunt,,
fuck her,,   the day she
            dies will be a great day;
Fuck you———. Go
            die you stupid
fucking   cunt. You can   burn
in hell right next to terrorist you
fucking   scum of a   human, @
——————;
—————— is a stupid
fuckin   cunt and   I hope she
            dies
#——————'s   full concession speech to quote
            Tupac:
"FUCK   YOU
            DIE SLOW."   #DemExit #ElectionFraud#Bernie;
            CUNT;
                I call upon ye GOD fear, Christian
                countrymen, if the liberals stick the
                whore—————in the White House,
                take yer guns,
            KILL THE CUNT
            DEAD!;
Ana Navarro shove your index finger up
        ——————'s cunt and keep on smelling the
        shit till you faint and
        drop dead until Huma Abedin's husband gives you the
                        Nobel Prize;
                #ThankYouBernie for
                showing me there IS
                a better way.

Fuck that   cunt———.
                              Hope she
           dies.
Fuck   ———. She's a
           cunt and   I hope she
           dies in a car accident.   #NotADemocrat;
G R A P H I C
      W A R N I N G !!!
                              I don't use this word often but
——— is a sick,pedavore,
CUNT! She needs to be
swinging from a tree!   LOCK HER UP before some
                                        good patriot
smashes her head on the s i d e w a l k.

Gal-vanized

We saw the news twenty minutes after the document leaked: "Supreme Court Set to Overturn *Roe v. Wade*." D sits in the armchair, reeling, reading article after article out loud, but before he even finishes the first paragraph, my brain is loud with a buzzing I can't shake. I feel gutted but grateful my partner can carry my anger for me for now.

I'm watching *The Real Housewives of Beverly Hills*, which seems like a bad joke during such a heavy moment. D reads the votes for the corresponding justices while Lisa Rinna makes up with Garcelle Beauvais. The two realities—one unfolding in front of Andy Cohen, one seeping out of my partner's mouth—feel like far-reaching foils to each other, or at least they could be, if I had heard anything at all.

When I went back to high school my senior year after having Beck, I walked down the halls with my head lowered, even though the predominantly conservative student body had applauded me for keeping the baby. In my twenties, I ran into one of those Republican girls at a bar, and she was drunk enough to tell me she was so thankful I didn't kill that baby as soon as I had found out.

She didn't know I had been labeled one of the most liberal students on the debate team, or how I felt like I didn't possess the autonomy to make a choice. She didn't know I felt happy I didn't have an abortion because I was grateful for the way my life turned out, and, to her, that would complicate me not being antiabortion.

Her rhetoric lacked the nuance needed to understand I simply got lucky. Social services and Medicaid, programs the conservative right wouldn't have a problem gutting, offered financial assistance to keep

Beck and me alive. I was fortunate my mother was there to help me with childcare and emotional support when I needed to work or go to school, or when I needed to struggle through waves of suicidal ideations and depressive lows I claimed were lukewarm but were, in fact, all-encompassing.

Today, it's more difficult to qualify for the aid low-income mothers need for bare-minimum survival. Not everyone has a mother who will stay with them.

*

The next morning, I open my phone and looked at anything but social media, even though my hands' muscle memory keep steering me toward Twitter and Instagram. I open an astrology app, putting my fate in the stars. Its advice for today: "Sometimes all you can do is absorb the shock."

The fifth month of this year, we're confronted with the collapse of *Roe v. Wade*, the continuation of a possible third world war, and layered episodes of gun violence punctuated with the second deadliest school shooting next to Sandy Hook. Our current landscape is a series of shocks that I don't know how to absorb—it's like Missouri in spring, when the ground is too wet to soak up the next rainstorm, causing floods across the state. We will get swept up in it all.

As a mother and as a human, I don't know how to feel galvanized again. By June, religious zealots flood street corners in my section of Missouri with signs for fetus rights. Two men pray violently over a homeless woman sitting on a street bench. The threat of disintegrating *Roe v. Wade* has caused the most righteous of these protestors to feel like their work has really done something, like the lady Beck and I pass every day on the way home from school. Her image is imprinted in my brain on nights when sleep doesn't come easy: a graying woman sitting on the other side of the gate at the Planned Parenthood, sign facing toward the building.

I saw her just yesterday. It was Beck's last day of sophomore year, and the sky was dark and bursting—just about to pour. It had already started to drizzle by the time we were almost home. The ground is full from last week's rain.

Step Six

How to Love Your Home

When someone asks where you're from, cringe dramatically if they respond with an emphatic "*Misery*???" How do you tell them that yes, it is a bit of misery, but it can also be something beautiful and something real? As you get older, you try to talk less shit about your home, especially when you're in front of your son, who you can feel retreating inside of himself out of guilt. For a lot of his life, you've talked about finally leaving this state once he is out of high school, realizing too late that these amassed side comments could compound into something that looked like resentment.

As a Black man, your partner doesn't feel safe here, but he reminds you that he doesn't feel safe anywhere. This won't make you feel better. Before the overturn of *Roe*, the two of you had thought about having a child, but in your mid-thirties, you'd qualify as a geriatric pregnancy and not having close access to a hospital could be dangerous if there were any complications. How do you find home in a place that is leading in book bans but has one of the laxest policies on gun regulation? Where your queer community is afraid of their rights being taken away every day? Don't forget how the people you found within these communities can make Missouri feel alive with possibility, full of hope.

Spoiler alert: Your partner ends up getting a tenure-track job in the heart of Missouri the same year your son turns eighteen. So you stay even longer, working toward finding things to love about your state in order to survive it. You'll both find that this home is easier to endure when you find someone worth staying for.

Two Degrees of Separation from Brad Pitt

When I first meet people and tell them where I'm from, a spark of hillbilly-rooted stereotypes flash across their eyes: an image of a car with a Confederate flag painted on the roof, Southern Baptists preachers waving at a gun show. You can nearly hear a faint echo of a drawl as thick as mud.

Before they can ask where my accent is, I let them know Brad Pitt is from the Ozarks, too — he's actually from my hometown. Suddenly I'm very popular and interesting and not a hillbilly at all. I wow them with the fact Brad Pitt's mom was my early childhood teacher, which means my Ozarks-ass is only a couple degrees away from a handsome man.

I gave Brad Pitt's mom a copy of *The Runaway Bunny* as a goodbye gift when I moved on to kindergarten. My mom ran into her while grocery shopping years ago, and she told my mom she still reads from that same copy to her grandkids.

There's a world where Brad Pitt opened a book in his mother's home and saw my name scribbled on the inside, and we are living in it.

When Natalie Walks into the Snow

We will think of Natalie walking into the snow during our own quiet moments, moments of unrest, pregnant with an ineffable hopelessness. We will think of how she thought she saw him swaddled against the magnolia tree, how its fresh blooms folded into the snow hitting its petals, making the night appear lighter, a little more alive than it had been only hours ago. *It must be him*, she will convince herself when she opens the door, alarmed by the handle's cold brass.

After all, it was early spring in Missouri—not the time and place for snow. *Surely, it must be him.*

Maybe Natalie woke up to the April snow. Perhaps her mother gave her Ambien to make sleep come more easily, the growing absence of thought comforting her to a temporary sanctuary where she wouldn't have to think of him like she had thought of him the last thirty-six hours. When she woke, the morning light would hit her face as she stepped out into an untouched dusting, the sun illuminating high cheekbones as her puffy eyes widened with the thought: *It must be him.*

Or maybe Natalie didn't sleep at all and she was already awake when the snow began to fall at four in the morning. Perhaps Natalie saw the slow flakes dancing above neighborhood streetlights from the kitchen sink, and we will picture her that moment when she first saw the snow. The image will follow us around for the next infinitude of weeks: Natalie, paralyzed at the kitchen sink, staring hard out the window in disbelief. Perhaps she went outside as soon as she saw the fresh blanket, running outside without her shoes, hypnotized. She will tell her home's remaining tenants, a grown golden retriever and newly adopted terrier mix, to wait inside as she walks into the snow.

We will speculate if Natalie noticed the cold at all. Perhaps the warmth of what the snow meant permitted her to say for the first time, "Thank you so much for seeing me. I see you, too." She will say it to the sky, to the moon's light obscured by low-hanging clouds. And she will scoop up the snow, her hands a bowl of stilled time, saying it again when she looks up to the magnolia tree: "Thank you so much," she will say. And again: "Thank you so much."

*

Beck and I eat in a dark Japanese restaurant, faces orange from the warm glow of offseason Christmas lights. He collects emptied edamame pods one by one until there is a small hill of green, a heap of empty shells.

I watch him. He's fascinating to watch. I like how his eyes survey the room, how I can tell when he questions something, his eyebrows doing all the talking. During these dinners, we chat about baseball, maybe how the Cardinals and the Cubs are neck and neck again for first in their division.

He's smarter than me, I'm always telling friends and family, even if they've heard me say if before. I repeat it partially because it's the truth but also because it carries a quiet subtext saying: "Look, everyone, anyone. I really can raise him effectively."

Beck still hasn't gotten the hang of chopsticks, so he forks the yellowtail nigiri frustrated, eyebrows narrowed. It's a different type of nigiri each time we go out. A few weeks ago, we tried eel. The time before was salmon roe — his favorite, he said to me, though it seems yellowtail is a close second. I can tell by the way he closes his eyes after the first bite, shakes his head "yes."

His dad won't take him out for sushi. His wife doesn't like seafood. And it's expensive. Beck points out the differences between his dad and me often. "Dad doesn't like to go to new places. He likes doing home improvement stuff," he told me while we drove through Kansas to spend a week in the Rockies with my cousin and his wife. Or, "Dad doesn't go on drives like you. He takes the direct way home." He has said this one many times. "Dad goes to church." It's a fun reminder of the good habits I promise to start, wishing that my brain could be steadier, more "normal." I wish I wasn't the type of person compelled to get sushi because *it's fun*, despite a dwindling bank account.

When these differences are mentioned, I will tell Beck that people like different things, they have different values. Even still, I feel like I am doing something wrong, and other people must be thinking I'm doing something wrong, too. For instance, there is the family of four sitting on the other side of the dark restaurant. A father and his oldest son around Beck's age — maybe eleven or twelve — sit side by side. The son is eating fried chicken while the mother disciplines the toddler daughter in a shush-shush church voice. The mother and father have a routine for dining out. This is clear when only the father speaks to the waiter and how the mother takes the girl to the bathroom to clean up when a spill occurs. *It's just water*, I think.

The mother notices me watching, giving me a sharp glance on her way to the bathroom. She holds her daughter's hand firm as the girl walks quickly to keep up with the steps. The mother's focus shifts to Beck, who is distracted by a phone notification. She frowns, and I feel like I'm doing something wrong again. I wonder if she is judging me for Beck being on his phone or for the simple fact that it is only the two of us. I wonder if she tried to gauge my age, a question which has followed me to every restaurant we go to.

I look down, clumsily grabbing the yellowtail with my chopsticks. The rice crumbles from a force that was too hard, too quick.

I try to brush it off, convincing myself it was just a look. Perhaps she was embarrassed by her loud child or perhaps she was jealous that Beck and I looked comfortable just being quiet.

But maybe we should be talking instead?

Unsettled, I decide on: "Hey."

He looks up, his eyebrows asking, "What?"

Less unsettled, I decide on: "Do you think it's meta to eat edamame with your mom?" I ask him.

"I think it's metamame," he says. He doesn't blink, doesn't skip a beat.

Our laughter is surely carried past the bathroom doors.

*

"I know you're inundated with messages right now," we will message Natalie. You tell her you have been thinking of her for the past hour, how no one ever really knows what to say in these moments. But she should know that when her world gets too quiet, someone will be thinking of her.

"Thank you for feeling this with me," Natalie will say a few days later. And this undoes us again. What we didn't say to Natalie: We read your post when we couldn't sleep, and when we got to the part about the snow, we felt a weight in our bodies that only comes with inexplicable grief. How could we tell a twenty-six-year-old widow that, just for a short amount of time, we could almost feel her in the early hours of the morning? How could we say: We saw you walking into the snow? We've seen her walking out into the snow a thousand times now. It feels rude to tell her how we can feel our hearts drop when we think of her and the snow and how she saw him in the snow. It looks self-righteous to say we saw even a glimpse of it because we could see ourselves in the snow, too. We're ashamed that we want to know if he left a note.

Our mothers have told us that we feel more than other people, and this carries a certain weight with it. There is a vibrant, infectious love where we can be moved to tears in an instant, like the time we watched a man get out of his car to help a boy on his way to the bus, the wind catching loose-leaf papers in his hands as the white sheets littered the yard. But then there are long periods where the national news will have us in bed for days, and this will spiral into "why?" which spirals into "why bother?" which spirals into "why am I here?" which spirals into "why?" again and stays with us indefinitely.

Our partners will try to remind us of how we also experience infectious love whenever they can feel a sense of dread coming to the surface. So we will try to get out of bed, and we will find small pride when we brush our teeth or take the dog out to go to the bathroom, just to implode all over again when we realize it's already June. Our partners will reassure us: "It's okay. There is still plenty of time."

These kinds of realizations dig deeper beneath our skin when we think of Natalie walking out into the snow because when we see Natalie, we're also seeing our partners, our sons and daughters, or our mothers who told us we felt too much. We will cry again, for Natalie and the snow and for him and for what our mothers may have said if it was one of us who finally gave way.

*

During our sushi dates, sometimes I look at Beck and pride and love and the capacity of time overcome me. I get anxious when this happens—talking fast, words running into one another. A doctor told me this is because my brain scurries when I think or feel too many things at the same time.

Beck can feel when I'm getting anxious. He knows the cues better than me. "Just breathe," he will tell me during these moments, and I will feel an equal sense of gratitude and shame. I'll never tell Beck how endless sleep feels like an offering of relief, and I worry the suicidal ideations are hereditary, praying that he doesn't have my genetics ripe with comorbid ADD and depression, anxiety for days. The ability to fold inside oneself.

The last time I thought about dying was a week before Natalie walked into the snow. We were sitting at our favorite restaurant—a small Italian chain found in Missouri. We had just dropped my partner off at the St. Louis airport after a weekend in Columbia, where he was visiting for a PhD reception for a program he'd be starting later in the fall.

Beck ran his teeth along stuffed artichoke leaves. It was his first solid food. I hardly remember this, and my body tightens with guilt when my mother tells the story to friends, family, maybe a stranger with a child on her hip. When I find myself feeling shame, my partner tells me to change the direction of my thoughts to something more positive. He hopes this will ultimately shape the pattern of my brain, but when my brain feels so scattered, I find little hope in any grounding.

His eyebrows were thoughtful. He asked, "How can I get into a school in Seattle?"

I was taken aback by the question—perhaps my partner's recent trip to a PhD program was fresh in his mind, or perhaps it was our family trip to Washington last month. Maybe it's because he loves *Frasier* so much (I wake up to him watching episodes before taking him to school in the morning).

I told Beck, "You're smart. You can go anywhere you want. You don't have to stay in Missouri."

The last part is bitter. I remembered the way he moaned when we landed in Kansas City, and he whispered underneath his breath, "Back in Missouri, I guess." It carried the same tone when I realized having a child meant staying in Missouri longer.

Beck's eyebrows grow deeper as he moves to another artichoke leaf. He said, "Okay."

I said, "You don't have to think about this now. You're only twelve."

He looked up—not what he was thinking. He asked, "Why didn't you go to school somewhere other than Missouri?"

The question brought me back five years. We were watching tv in the living room and a commercial came on encouraging viewers to donate to a West African adoption facility. Images of underweight children flooded the screen. A woman's voice gives the audience statistics of hunger, poverty, and a lack of education.

After, Beck glanced over at me. "Thank you for keeping me," he said.

I wish there was a way to tell him that he was the one who saved me, who stayed with me so I stayed for him.

Five years later, in a booth in a small Missouri town on the way back home, I tightened my lips, just like after I did after the commercial. I told him, "Because I had you."

He tightened his lips, too. "Oh," he said.

And I said, "No. No, no." I said: "I wouldn't have had it any other way." And he knew I meant it because I don't lie well. My emotions and eyebrows always give me away.

Beck smiled, squeezing a lemon wedge into a fresh glass of sweet tea. For a flash, his eyebrows looked too adult, and I saw a glimpse of what he would look like as an adult. I've only experienced this one time before, during a trip to the Rockies the summer before. I had surprised Beck with Beck tickets—another meta joke we share. There was a light rain at Red Rocks, the kind of pop-up storm that only happens in the foothills of the mountains.

Following my cousin, I realized I had lost track of my son while going through security. My cheeks grew red, I could feel the anxiety even in that soft rain. There were only a few seconds of panic, and then my eyes settled on him. A hoodie covered his head, dirty-blond hair—our hair—peeking out, not yet damp enough to stick to his forehead. The hoodie used to be too tight, but he had grown a billion inches in the last few months, and his stomach and legs had thinned. He didn't see me at first, too preoccupied with a security checkpoint. The security guard asked him something, and he didn't have to look up because he was already her height, maybe five-five or five-six. He smiled to the security guard. A matter-of-fact smile, as his palm hit hers in the air—a hip high-five.

Everything grew quiet. Time had both stilled and fast-forwarded into an ineffable moment when I saw my son in the Rocky Mountain rain, and he was both twelve and twenty-four years old. I couldn't hear the thousands of people speaking around me or how there was a faint smell of marijuana in the air, and I didn't notice that the rain was coming down heavier or how there were glow lights being sold from carts even though it wasn't quite dusk yet. I couldn't even hear my own thoughts, which were usually louder than everything.

Then he looked over, saw me in the rain staring at him and gave me a smile that I recognized. The moment flickered, and he was a boy once more.

*

We will think of our own mothers and partners when we think of Natalie walking out to the snow. We will think of the places and the moments that they may find us. Your mother would have found you in the water, the only place you felt at home. She'd collapse from the memory of calling you a fish when you moved past your brother during swimming lessons. A little on the nose for being a Pisces, but you didn't care as long as you were in the water. Another memory: you at three years old, crying to go farther into Lake Michigan because a hundred feet and the sandbar weren't far enough. Maybe she'd remember the way she would dive into a pool, feet up in the air — a beckoning for you to hold onto — and she'd dive into the water once she felt your arms around her legs. A whale and her calf, she called it.

Even as a child, you appreciated the kind of silence brought with immersing yourself in water. Other children would ask why you opened your eyes underneath the surface. "There's nothing to see," some would say. You liked the way the sun hit the edge of the water, spreading its rays like a sea urchin made of light. You loved how your hands looked pushing against the density, how the water felt like a baptism each time you held your breath.

Your son would find you during the golden hour. He'll be sixteen in three years, and surely he will be partial to Ozarks' drives when he feels lost. He'd remember drives during your own lost moments, how each time the sun began to set, there was that warm light spreading across the Missouri hills. You'd say to him, "Look up from your book. This is the golden hour. Everything is a little more beautiful during the golden hour." And maybe the golden hour at sixteen would somehow bring him back to that first day of being, how he cried until the nurse put him in your arms, and once he was there, you closed your eyes and he must have closed his eyes too, because there was a small instant of basking silence, the halogen lights warming your faces just like that golden hour glow. You want him so badly to not be like you, that feeling so much isn't worth the risk of wanting to shut it all off, forever.

*

We will say sorry when Natalie walks into the snow, and we will say a prayer just low enough she would brush the whisper aside as a morning dove greeting the budding dawn. Or: *Maybe it's the wind*, she would think. *Maybe it's him again*, she would hope. And it's better for her to have that soft hope, an invocation she holds in her hands, than for her to know it came from a lineup of people who felt just as lost as her husband. We've thought about leaving again and again. Maybe one of us was just thinking it before we read her post about the snow. We wouldn't want to imply that it could have been any one of us instead, because then she would ask, "Would he still be there if another wife saw her dead husband in the snow?"

Instead, we will cry with her, and we will say sorry over and over again, the April snow crunching beneath our feet.

Penumbra

FARMINGTON, MISSOURI
37°46'51" N, 90°25'18" W
21 AUG 2017
FIRST CONTACT: 11:49:56 AM CDT

Before birdsongs waned, Beck pointed to the sky, said, *Look. It's starting.* So I looked past his finger and toward the starting sky. If a cardinal had flown by, she would have looked twice, unsure of what she had seen — the two of us looking up and into her world, eyes protected behind cheap paper glasses with special black lenses. The bird would have seen the others gaze with us: Sierra and Liv, airport workers, the wealthy families who arrived in small planes. A flock of cartoon sunglasses + the lone air traffic controller sporting a welding mask he brought from home.

But there weren't any birds in the sky when Beck pointed to it and said, *Look. It's starting,* because the birds had already felt a shift in the tropospheric air. Instead, they stayed in trees surrounding the small Ozarks airport, eavesdropping in on our conversations, like when Beck, still looking up, asked, *When does it start?*

Liv answered, *A little past one.* Beck frowned. They reassured Beck: *There are other things to see before.*

And I said, *Like the shadows.*

Beck repeated, *Like the shadows.*

The bird would have heard the people from small airplanes discussing sky routes toward home once there was nothing left to see, not even sunlit patches in the of shape crescent moons, moon-obstructed sunbeams that littered the shadows as the two spheres nudged toward one another.

Another conversation for the birds: Sierra introducing me to an airport worker. Her father. He would tell me he's heard a lot about me from Sierra's tales of graduate office laughs. Sierra said, *She's my Mama Bird*, and I looked at her father and he looked at me. We had taken our cartoon sunglasses off, so he could read me hard if he was the kind of person to read people well. I attempted a clumsy smile that tried to say, *You're daughter has been a good friend to me.*

Maybe the birds wouldn't have listened at all because they had already seen Beck pointing to the sky, reading his mouth forming into the words: *Look* and *it's* and *starting*. From the trees they looked with us, together with Liv and Sierra and airport workers and the people from small planes who the birds recognized from the sky.

_____( )_____( )_____

ALPENA, MICHIGAN
45°3'42"N, 83°25'58"W
03 JULY 2017
"ECLIPSE 2017: THE GREATEST EVENT OF OUR LIFETIMES!"
START TIME: 3:00:00 PM EDT

During a vacation to her home state, my mother drove Beck and me to a planetarium on the tip of Michigan's mittened pointer finger. A graduate student used a laser to guide his audience's attention to projected images on the domed ceiling. Heads tilted toward a superimposed night sky, our eyes follow the red dot as we learned about the history of the sun and the moon folding together.

The graduate student spends time introducing the audience to Rahu, a Hindu demon who defied all pre-history when he took a swig of an elixir offering immortality. Surya and Chandra—sun and moon—catch Rahu's act. For punishment, Vishnu cut off Rahu's head, his mortal body disintegrating into time while a disembodied noggin lives on, its cheeks flushed with anger as it forever chases skyballs in retribution. We will see the moment Rahu catches up. We will see him eat the sun or the moon with haste. But he won't be able to lift the spheres up to his mouth without hands. In a solar eclipse, we will see Surya carry on her way, the world returning to light for those of us watching from the ground.

Other noted cultural interpretations of celestial hunger:

>Dragon, China
>Sibling Skywolves, Norse Mythology
>Milky-Way-Strolling Bear, Pomo Tribe
>Apep, a chaos and death snake, Egypt Fire Dogs, Korea
>   a Big Ass Sky Frog in Vietnam

My mother's breathing got heavier as the graduate student moved from beasts in the heavens to gods. He explained how twenty-five hundred years ago, the eclipse of Thales occurred during a battle between the Medes and Lydians. As the moon covered the sun, the world darkened and both sides stared up at the sky and then to each other, spears lowering at each man's side. The eclipse was read as an omen from the gods, a demand to stop fighting. So they did, ending a war that had lasted for fifteen years.

The projector moves onto an image of this year's eclipse. The red light now trails the width of the United States, Oregon to South Carolina.

Totality, he said. The half of the audience who is awake learned Alpena, Michigan wouldn't be in the line of totality, but its residents could still experience a partial solar eclipse. *The penumbra*, he explained. The sky still becomes dark, and the air cooler. The birds will still quiet out of confusion.

Beck leaned over, whispered, *Hey*. He waves his hand and points to Missouri, where totality will hit three hours north of our home in Springfield. *Can we go?*

We'll see. You'd be missing school, I told him, knowing already that we'd be going home with two pairs of solar glasses from the planetarium gift shop.

_____( )_____( )_____

SPRINGFIELD, MISSOURI
37°12'32" N, 93°17'32" W
XX NOVEMBER 2017
MIDDLE-OF-SHIFT: 06:XX:XX PM CDT

The woman tells me she likes pink — really anything bright and colorful. *I'm not my mother*, she says.

Me, too, I say. She laughs with her eyes closed, missing my frown as I realize my syntactic ambiguity. But the woman never asks for clarification — if I meant her mother or my own. I try to move forward, bra-trajectory colored in pink and mapped with corresponding adjectives: Sensuous, Enticing, Stunning, Embraceable. She's eyeing the sea foam green balconet which promises to erase her back fat. Corresponding adjective: Vanishing.

I may have that one in fuschia. I smile the words, eyebrows raised.

She says, *Okay*. She says, *Okay*, again. She looks at the bra laying in her hands. *I think I need to be sized.*

All women look nervous when asking for a fitting. To be sized means to be mostly naked in front of a stranger, and we are prone to think strangers are always sizing us up in other ways: hip circumference, breast density, the way she paints her face. We are prone to think strangers are always sizing us up in all ways.

I tell her, *No problem*, and guide her to the fitting rooms in the back of the store. I ask her to go to the last one on the left. *The biggest one*, I tell her. I offer: *I can measure you in a tank top if that's more comfortable for you.*

The woman's speech becomes fast in between the ends and beginnings of sentences. She tells me she is from Arizona, but that she's been all over. She's seen the world during her time in the army. She hung out with Elton John at a bar once. This makes her laugh. She smiles through her words. I've learned people speak too much when they feel uncomfortable, but I don't mind listening to whatever she has to say. *Whatever you do with your money*, she says, *make sure you save enough of it to see whatever you can of the world.*

I'm trying, I say. I blink, ending the moment. *I'm going to measure your band first*, I tell her.

The measuring tape goes just below her breasts. Her arms hang along straight hips and into her large but delicate hands. I notice two large rings with familiar stones. She catches me looking at her hands. She misreads my stare and shifts her weight, hiding her hands behind her back. I noticed my hips doubling over hers in the mirror and move away from my own reflection.

But I need her hands to measure her cup size, or I've at least been told to ask women to hold the tape over the largest part of their bust. This makes them feel included, less exposed. When I ask her to hold the tape, she says, *Okay*, but her fingers are shy, moving slowly from the safe haven of concealment.

There is a peculiar intimacy which happens between strangers in fitting rooms. When I ask for her hands, that intimacy is clouded with an air of shame, perhaps betrayal. I try to be encouraging, to put on a more genuine smile than the one I greeted her with at the front door.

I say, *Yes, like that*. I notice her rings again, debate whether I should draw attention to her hands or if it's too risky.

I take the risk, eyes nodding toward her hands. People who wear stones love talking about them: the jewelry's history, the metaphysical meaning of the mineral, its geological significance, whether said stone is a particular favorite.

Turquoise?

She relaxes a little. *Yes*, she says. *It reminds me of home.* She explains turquoise is sold everywhere in Arizona—gas stations, Native American casinos, the gift shop at the mouth of the Grand Canyon. She confirms it's her favorite: *a Protection Stone.*

I smile at her hands. I tell her I'm jealous. And I am—the two rings are intricate in their silver design framing each large stone. I've seen similar pieces in glass classes with a price tag I could never afford.

To make her feel less seen, I hold out my own hand, embarrassed at my fingers—too short, stubby from years of popping knuckles when anxious. *This ring is moldavite*, I say. *If you hold it to the light, you can see wrinkles. You can see that it's actually green.* I take it off, holding it between my thumb and point finger. My fingernails are shit, unlike hers, which are polished and cuticle free, but the Moldavite looks green under the fluorescent lights just like I promised, and that makes the few seconds feel right enough. She says, *Pretty. Wasn't expecting that.*

I don't mention that moldavite is only found in Bohemian areas, forming its structure over time from a meteorite impact over fifteen million years ago, nor do I tell her how moldavite and turquoise are two different crystal classes entirely. The only chemical component they have in common is oxygen. All that really matters is they are both minerals at the beginning of the day, the end of it.

I tell her a number and a letter—her size.
 I used to be a 34, she says. *I figured the DDs wouldn't change though.*
 I say, *The average band width is 36.*
 She says, *Oh, good*, and lets out an air of relief.

I tell her I will bring some bright and loud bras—bras that would make her mother clutch her pearls. When I turn to open the door, she says to my back, *You know, I'm not like most women.*
 Her words are quick. They run into each other. I look back to her, my hand on the door. I say, *Me, too*, again.

She laughs, nervous still. I smile and shut the door on my way out. My brain circles back to linguistics, the perpetual syntactic and lexical ambiguity of words like "not" and "most" and "women" because of external normative standards and the weight of a woman's interiority. I wonder if most women feel like they aren't most women, and where does a question like that leave us? Perhaps with our eyes to the ground, which is where I imagine the woman in the dressing room is looking now.

I knock on the dressing room door and hand her a fuchsia bra that will take away the back fat she hardly has. Her hands take the bra from my hands. I watch the exchange, then I look up, then I see her. *No one can really say what "most women" means.* I look at her until she breaks eye contact, smiling at the open space between my body and hers.

She says, *Thank you.*

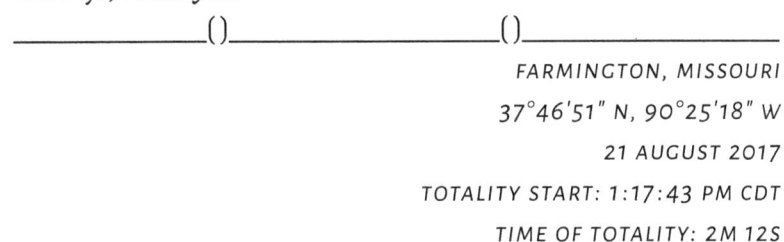

_____()_____()_____

FARMINGTON, MISSOURI
37°46'51" N, 90°25'18" W
21 AUGUST 2017
TOTALITY START: 1:17:43 PM CDT
TIME OF TOTALITY: 2M 12S

The birds were getting quiet. Beck looked at me, said, *The birds were getting quiet*, and he was right. The birds were getting quiet. As the moon wholly enveloped the sun, the birds hushed completely, their world and our world going dark in the time it takes to breathe without remembering, the time it takes to be unfazed by a bird's song on any other day. I reminded him of what the graduate student in the planetarium said about changes in the world's color, it's sharpening of shadows.

He asked, *How long do we have?* He waves his arms, his Peter Pan shadow waves with him, the silhouette so clear I could see the hairs on the shadow's arms.

Two minutes.

Liv said, *It's starting.* The stars blinked into the middle of the afternoon. The daybirds remained inaudible. An owl hooted. For two minutes and some change, we could stare at the sun without her hurting our eyes. Shadow bands appeared on the runway, snakes of light weaving along the cement.

When the sun reemerged, the day birds paused. They were confused, skeptical. We paused, too. We weren't confused or skeptical—both the graduate student and media sensationalism told us everything we could expect before, during, and after totality. Perhaps we paused because the moment after an eclipse offers a different kind of quiet, and you don't think of things like "us" or "them" during totality. You don't think about "me." Maybe we were all trying to hang on to those two minutes and some change as we stared up and around, together and apart. After all, we talked about the things we saw during our two minutes and change spent with the merging of the sun and the moon. We would all nod our heads hard, *Yes, that did happen!* And I remember how, during the first few seconds/millennia of the eclipse, I heard Beck gasp—a sharp intake of breath that must only happen when lights go out in the middle of the day. And I remember hearing someone cry. Sierra—and I loved her for offering tears. I remember Liv laying down on the landing strip, hands folded underneath their head, the way Beck quickly followed their lead.

Maybe then... well, maybe then I was wrong. I noticed everything about them—how I knew it was Sierra crying because when you know a person's essence, you'll likely know the pattern of their tears. And I remembered how, somehow, I noticed everything Beck did, and now I'm wondering what I noticed more. Was my attention on the sunbeams escaping the moon, the changes in the world around me, or how my son responded to it all? And when I will come to think of the eclipse in the following months and the following lifetime, I will always remember the way the world turned dark and how the birds grew quiet, but the sharper shadows of memory would hold the sound of Sierra weeping, the image of Liv and Beck, elbows in the air, heads resting on fingers, staring up into the sky as it faded back to day. I will remember his gasp during the first second of our holy minutes and change.

And the conversations that followed:

    How Sierra would say she cried.

How I smiled, how I said, *Yes, I knew that was you.* And I'd always remember how she smiled back because, damn, how beautiful it is to know someone's tears.

And how Liv said they just wanted to stare at the sky when they knew it was almost over so they stretched their body on the ground, shadow bands weaving around them.

And how Beck responded, *Yes—me, too!*

And how I laughed again, saying how I saw all of this, all of them.

And how everyone was a little sad, even the people from sky as they climbed up into their small airplanes. They nodded before shutting the door, saying, *Thanks.* And we nodded back, saying and giving our own thanks.

I'll remember how Beck squinted up at the normal sky before we went back home, the sun's light warm yet unfamiliar. He said to the sun, *Two minutes.* And he repeated it again: *Two minutes.*

He said, *The next time I think of two minutes, I will think of this eclipse.*

——————————(( ))——————————

OUTSIDE OF FARMINGTON, ST. JOE STATE PARK

37°48'15"N, 90°31'01"W

21 AUGUST 2017

TOTALITY START: 1:17:43 PM CDT

TIME OF TOTALITY: 2M 12S

An owl hooted, *The stars are out now.* Perhaps the hoot was to acknowledge how the birds were no longer talking.

The graduate student told Beck and me and my sleeping mother that it's not only daybirds who change their activity during an eclipse. There are also predatory birds, birds like owls, who will emerge hours before their usual wake time.

Though I never saw the owls come out in Farmington, 37°46'51"N, 90°25'18"W, I knew their hoots welcomed the early night all over Missouri, as if to say, "This eclipse affects us, too."

_____(( )_____

SPRINGFIELD, MISSOURI
37°12'32"N, 93°17'32"W
XX NOVEMBER 2017
MIDDLE-OF-SHIFT: 06:XX:XX PM CDT

At the register, I scan the woman's items — enough to make a bouquet of bright bras. She tells me again it's important to see as much of this world as I can. *If you have kids, show them the value of traveling, too.*

I tell her that I'm trying — that I'm doing what I can. She asks how old. I say nearly twelve. I look down at the computer screen, feigning a double check of her purchases. I can feel her looking at me, studying the age of my skin. She doesn't ask how old I am.

Instead, she leans over with her hand on the counter. She says, *I want you to know you're beautiful. Really. Beautiful. I hope you find someone who treats you beautifully.*

My first instinct is to reach for her hands. I nearly sob. My second instinct is to talk about the eclipse, to share what was remembered. I spend the rest of my shift thinking about penumbras, about the space in between and just out of reach, where birds grow too chatty or too silent because of the unfamiliar. I think about what it means to be seen vs. feel exposed, and how exhausting balancing that line must be for a woman who feels compelled to hide her hands.

This need to be seen is an idea I mull over often. I've heard someone argue that acknowledgement stems from an inerasable narcissism. Hegel would argue that self-awareness can only be gained through mutual recognition of two self-consciousness, but this recognition always arises from competition rather than camaraderie. Could recognition be synonymous with the innate need to love and be loved because we are all benefactors of our own personal pains and joys. Judith Butler describes love as neither a state nor a feeling. Rather, "Love is an exchange, uneven, fraught with history, with ghosts, with longings that are more or less legible to those who try to see one another with their own faulty vision."

When I nearly reached for the woman's hands, perhaps it came from a pure recognition, overcome by how two strangers found mutual gratitude in the span of a bouquet of colorful brassieres because, for a moment, they were both seen without the Other feeling the need to look away.

At the cash register, I'm not reflecting on Judith Butler's approach on love, nor am I thinking of how this transaction will push me to the next level of dogshit commission. I hand her a receipt. I wonder what two minutes means to her.

I say, *I hope you find the same. That someone treats you beautifully*. The words feel empty coming out as a response, a speech bubble with too much white space. Any sentiment I offered would bear the weight of words borrowed, merely reactive.

I try again: *Beautiful people deserve to be treated with beauty*.

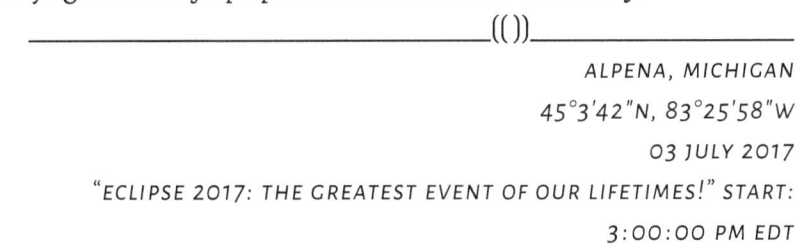

———————————————————(( ))———————————————

ALPENA, MICHIGAN
45°3'42"N, 83°25'58"W
03 JULY 2017
"ECLIPSE 2017: THE GREATEST EVENT OF OUR LIFETIMES!" START:
3:00:00 PM EDT

The graduate student explained solar eclipses weren't always about hungry skywolves or disappointed gods. Some believed the alignment of the sun and the moon suggested a fight in the heavens, a bickering brother and sister, a feuding husband and wife.

Batammaliba people in Togo and Benin attempted to reconcile the supernal dispute between the sun and moon with the only tools they could offer from the ground: through reconsideration of their own differences, then through meaningful conversation. A man apologizes to his neighbor, a woman let's go of her tightly held anger. They all smile, they nod.

They see each other's sadness and try to offer some healing. Perhaps in the end, they will no longer walk around each other, tiptoeing, eyes to the ground.

Their actions spoke upwards, urgent yet kind:

Sun and Moon, be like us. Sun, Moon — if we can let go, surely you can, too.

The sun will notice their effort first, gesturing with a solar-flared finger toward Earth for the moon to see.

The sun will say, *Look. It's starting.*

And the Moon will look past the Sun's finger beams and toward something new: toward a starting world.

D Explains How to Speak to a Police Officer

"When a cop comes to your window, keep your hands on the wheel," D says. "Be respectful. Say, 'Yes, sir,' or 'No, sir.' 'Yes, ma'am,' 'No, ma'am.'"

It's fall, and D is visiting from South Carolina. We're driving back from Nashville toward my home in Missouri, a state flagged by the NAACP with a travel warning for people of color. D has mentioned his fear of my home state more than once.

I want to alleviate his fear, so I say, "Okay, I'll try."

D says, "No. Do." His usual gentle inflection has been replaced with clipped tones.

I say, "Okay."

D tells me if we ever get pulled over, I will be angry at how the police officer talks to him.

His voice becomes sharp, his words faster: "You can't be poppin' off on a police officer."

I tell him I won't show my anger.

He says good.

I think, *What a weird power dynamic.*

I say, "What a weird power dynamic."

He stares out the window. "I know."

As the conversation fades out the open windows, I think about what D might have been like as a teenager, if he carried the weight of quiet anger the way he does now, his shoulders tense, posture guarded. I wonder when he learned the cadence of a soft speaker, or if it was always there out of necessity.

I can't shake the sharpness in his voice. I heard it once before, only a handful of months before, when he asked me: *Have you ever dated a Black man?* It was there for the question that followed too: *Are you ready to date a Black man?*

*

I remember our conversation again in winter, when we hear Shavahn Dorris-Jefferson read her poem "The Talk," structured as epistolary instructions to her son about how to talk to a police officer when he gets pulled over. There's not a question of if. She asks her son to please do whatever the officer says. She says put both hands on the wheel. She instructs him to say, "Yes, sir" and "No, sir." "Yes, ma'am," "No, ma'am." She begs him to please just make it home.

Her son is in the audience, just a few rows in front of us. He's a toddler. As his mother reads, the boy sits in his father's lap and plays with a phone, unaware.

After the reading, I ask D if his mother gave him a similar talk. "Of course," he says. All Black parents have that talk with their children.

I think of my white son, Beck, two years shy of sixteen. How the absence of a similar conversation between him and me was the root of its necessity for D and his mother. I tell myself to remember D's words. Conceal potential anger, redirect indignation from my throat to my hands on the wheel. Transform defensiveness into succinct politeness. Yes, sir. No, ma'am. *Please just let us get back home.*

*

When D visits Missouri again, it is early spring. We get sushi with Beck. We pick up a few things at the grocery store. D buys flowers—daisies, some speckled lilies. He says, "I thought you'd like the lilies." My eyes feel full. He tells me happy birthday.

On the way home, we stop at an intersection. There's a vehicle facing us, just stopped. It's a cop. The air grows thin. The cop is turning where we're turning, but, though he has the right-of-way and traffic is slow, he continues to wait. I try to remember what D said, but as soon as the blue lights come on, I forget all of it fumbling for my wallet.

D asks if I have a way to contact his sister in case anything happens. His voice is sharp and quick. He's right beside me, but his body feels out of reach.

I say, "But you haven't done anything wrong."

And D repeats, "Do you have my sister's contact information." I tell him I think so. Beck is quiet in the back seat.

The officer walks to my window. He says he pulled me over because my front plate is displayed incorrectly. I tell him my car isn't manufactured with a front plate mount. I think about the number of times a police officer has driven past me without caring that my plate is on the dash of the car.

He asks for my license, and I hand it to him silently. He says, "And sir, can you hand over your license too?" D says a few words, and the officer is visibly surprised by his voice—hushed, polite. Perhaps he will think he made a mistake.

My anxiety surges when I realize I didn't say *sir*, when I realize I did none of the things D instructed me to do. But D was wrong about me getting angry. Instead I go lightheaded with fear when the officer tells me to step outside of the vehicle.

*

The officer lets me sit in the front seat, and my anger appears at last. This same kindness wouldn't have been extended to D. The officer says I really should have gone to court after I got that ticket for expired tags six months ago. "But it helps you've never been arrested before." In fact, I'd called the municipal court to confirm my court date, but when they couldn't find my name in their system, I assumed—I felt free to assume—that I'd gotten lucky. But I say none of this. My mind keeps drifting back to how the officer who gave me that ticket six months ago hardly noticed the white male friend sitting in my passenger's seat.

Several hours later D picks me up at the corrections facility. He wraps his arms around me, laughing as he says, "I don't think the officer expected this to turn out the way it did." I smile. I cry. I say it's not fair. On the drive home, I look over at D and say I'm sorry again and again, the words spilling out as we drive past city hall, past the spaces that allowed me to assume and to forget. In a month, a mug shot will pop up first when someone googles my name. I look disheveled from having to take out my ponytail. I'm tired and angry, and there's a hardness in my eyes, my jaw tense from gritting my teeth.

All Things Being Equal

When I tell my mom that the Arkansas art museum is opening to members for private viewing, she offers to put us up in a hotel. She says she's been worried about D these past few weeks, and it's the least she can do. To make her feel better, I tell her we'll think about it.

D and I do the math later in the evening, calculating the expense of gas and food and debating whether it is worth a few hours of peace. I say it may be nice to see the Hank Willis Thomas exhibit again, pointing out how we felt rushed with the amount of people on Valentine's Day. I add, "It may feel powerful to see it, considering everything happening."

D says okay, as long as Beck is interested in going again.

Over Instagram, I ask my fourteen-year-old if he's down to see Crystal Bridges in a couple days. He responds, "Bet," and I have to ask D if this means yes. D nods, laughing, and for a moment, the weight of the protests and blacked out social media feeds isn't clinging to the conversation. For a handful of seconds, my mind isn't lingering on the dangers that come with D being a Black man in Missouri.

Before dating D, I never recognized the way white people could overcompensate out of guilt, or the amount of microaggressions that come with any given outing. As a white person, I convinced myself I never needed to. Now, it's less often he'll need to point out these moments, which even follow us to the quiet visit to Crystal Bridges. On our way in, a couple in their seventies is leaving, and as we approach, their eyes move toward D. The woman smiles hard beneath her mask, enough to make the fabric move with her mouth. White people have been smiling at D a lot lately. Though it's not necessarily wanted, the attention that comes with white guilt is preferred to the microaggressions—moments like when the security guard sees us and nods, but then hesitates as we continue our way to the front doors. We've already walked past him when he tells us it's members only today. We turn around, confirm we are, in fact, members. Even then, his eyebrows narrow. Soon enough he will see our reserved tickets confirmed at the entrance.

I sigh a big, "Wowwwwww."

Beck asks why the security guard questioned us.

D laughs—says it's because we don't look like anyone else here. "I like that we don't look like anyone here," he adds. "It's kind of cool."

But the security guard gets under my skin, his question carrying with me through the museum as we cross paths with other members—all of them over sixty and white. Some smile beneath masks, and we smile back. Their gaze doesn't recoil out of apology when our eyes meet. Under some masks, lips tighten, as if asking who we are—what was our story? The answer is two Ph.D. students and our son. The answer is a family trying to find some breath.

The stares are the most obvious in the Hank Willis Thomas exhibit, *All Things Being Equal*. One installation consists of five televisions. James Baldwin flickers across the screens, sometimes separately, sometimes all at once. We sit six feet away from woman already watching; another woman joins, standing off to side. Together, we watch the James Baldwins reflect on being Black in America. When the screens grow quiet, the Baldwins sigh, each taking a puff of his cigarette. I notice how each woman, at some point, glances in D's direction, perhaps half out of apology, perhaps half out of wondering what is going through his mind.

The three of us break off in the next part of the Thomas exhibit. D drifts toward the pieces encouraging flash photography. I hear an attendant explain how, if he takes a photo with flash, the photo will reveal parts of a narrative previously invisible. On the surface, one piece shows a Black protestor standing still, both hands offering a peace sign. The flash of a camera reveals police in full military garb, restraining two German Shepherds lunging, teeth bared.

On the other side, I catch Beck staring at *Two Little Prisoners*, which is a simple but unnerving design. The piece is a large mirror with a superimposed image of a police officer kneeling beside two Black boys — one holding a crime booking card, which reads "24841." Beck's face hovers just above the boys' faces, and he studies his reflection implicated in its history. Until he catches me watching him. Through the mirror, he looks back at me and waves.

*

The security guard nods again whenever we make our way back to the car. I try not to carry the irritation with me on the drive back home. Instead, the three of us each take turns with our favorite art of the day.

When I ask D if it was worth the trip, he says, "Definitely," without a pause.

Over the next few weeks, conversations surrounding the protests and police militarization will grow heavier, and I will find myself going back to our car ride home — a reminder that, even in the midst of amassing chaos and rising tension, my partner can find moments of definite peace. And that's reason enough to push through to the next day, and the days that follow, in hopes that conversations won't be forgotten — in hopes we continue to learn.

Homecoming

We never saw the call coming, but we'd always known it was a possibility. It was a possibility for any parent. In the midst of toilet paper shortages and loaded Missouri masking policies, I had forgotten the shape of pre-pandemic anxieties.

*

The theme, "masquerade," was in the back of our minds as we shopped for Beck's first high school dance. He told D and me how homecoming court was gender-neutral this year, how one person would represent homecoming royalty.

D and I are surprised by this. We both ask, "Really?" in disbelief—not because we're dismissive of gender fluidity, but because we live in Missouri, where megachurches encourage thousands to vote against antidiscrimination ordinances and the election county map is so red it looks like we're sinking in lava, save for the handful of blue lakes sprinkled here and there. All in the northern part of the state. If we drive fifteen minutes out of town, D gets nervous from the way people look at us, as if we've assaulted them with our interracial partnership. He tells me not to stare back if anyone watches without apology. I can feel their eyeballs burn into our skulls while pumping gas or even as we pass by on the road. Confederate flags and billboards for gun shows within every twenty miles.

Still, we are in the city of Columbia, a small blue area between St. Louis and Kansas City. Diversity is relatively present here. D isn't the only Black person in the grocery store. Beck's high school is only 65 percent white. It's a much different vibe than his last school in southwest Missouri, which was 91 percent white and parents predominantly pro-Trump. Gender inclusivity wasn't included in their homecoming vocabulary. It wasn't included in any high school within Christian County.

I try not to think about demographics. After all, Beck was here now — he said he was happier, and he was making friends. It was a relief just to see him looking forward to anything after this last year. To distract myself, I ask what he's thinking for an outfit.

Unsurprisingly, he already has a clear vision. All black, including his mask. "Like one of those plague doctors from the Middle Ages, if we can find one." *The Medico della Peste.*

It's close to Halloween and masks are readily available — a relief since we missed the window to order online. The Halloween store parking lot is flooded with high school students, walking in groups toward the entrance decorated with an orange banner and a grim reaper welcoming each guest. Their conversations carry over our music in the car.

Beck and D look nervously at me when they see the crowd. D says maybe I should wait in the car.

Beck agrees: "Probably a good idea,"

For a moment, I'm suspended between gratefulness and shame. Since the pandemic, my social anxiety has hit an apex that still hasn't settled much. D calls it agoraphobia, but that doesn't explain wanting to see people but not knowing how. It doesn't explain my back roads drives lasting upward of an hour. I'll take them whenever our home feels in a state of unrest, whether from silence or too much noise. Unrest seems to be happening a lot this past year and a half, but it's calmed since Beck has moved in full-time.

Later, I'll feel guilty I didn't go in. I'll think to ask if people ever give strange looks at D and Beck when they're together and I'm not there.

"Always," D says, "but less when we're on the coasts." His PhD defense is next month, but we'll be staying in Missouri for another three years while Beck and I finish school. Every time I think of my home state, I think of D's discomfort here. It's a weight I know I'll feel until we can move somewhere safer, until we finally find a new place to call home.

*

Homecoming is under a tent outside this year, allowing students to replace their typical mandated canvas face masks with ones decorated in sequins and feathers, glitter outlining the shape of their face and eyes. After the Halloween shop, we move to the mall. I amp myself up to go in. Whether it's the guilt from staying in the car the first time or the need to show my family I'm doing better, I force myself to get out of the car. In either case, I'm galvanized enough to make it past Spencer's and the food court and into H&M. I can hear each conversation along the way, compounded into one pervasive buzz, growing louder with each step. I keep my head tilted toward the ground, three feet in front of us. If I allow myself to look up, for my eyes to survey the waves of the crowd, their faces may meld together, too. Instead, I'll steal a glance from D and feign a smile hidden underneath thermoplastic polymer. I give a silent thanks for the face mask—the gesture wasn't believable, but I had convinced myself it was good enough.

Beck looks for a black button up. D tells me to let him do his thing, but I need a distraction from the fact we are the only people in the store wearing masks, despite the sign outside saying they're required for entry. I sort through cheap but fashionable sweaters to keep me busy. My mind shifts from the pastel hoodies to a picture of what homecoming may look like tonight: a swarm of students dancing underneath the tent, singing along to a crowd favorite. An ocean of anonymity and glitter. Perhaps "American Boy," a throwback from Estelle featuring Kanye is playing, or maybe they'll hum along with Cudi's "The Void." It'll be hot under the tent, but that's okay. The fact that homecoming is even happening at all is enough to get over the muggy Midwestern heat. An image flashes of teenagers being quietly shocked by the presence of their peers' mouths, thankful for their masks and the darkness to conceal wide eyes and raised eyebrows. I laugh to myself at the thought, but it comes out too loud because of the nerves.

Beck shoots a look that's sharp, but with a hint of vulnerability. "What?" he mouths from across the room.

I brush it off, shaking my head. I wave "nothing" with my right hand, remembering the danger of teenage sensitivity. Emotions are ferocious when convincing yourself you're made of steel.

*

Just a year before, I had new worries amassing on top of the coronavirus. I started a PhD program that fall. My dog was slowly dying. And I was in a custody battle I could hardly process. Most of the year was spent in my head, thoughts racing to the point of dizziness. Even during sleep, I was in a state of unrest, often waking up with my heart beating in my throat.

By January 2021, most of these problems would find some sense of closure. My dog passed away a few days after the New Year. Right before February, I got a call from my lawyer saying Beck's dad was willing to settle, allowing Beck to choose where he wanted to live. In spring, I'd still have the weight of teaching and graduate classes but opted to focus on mental health and would take a leave of absence the following academic year.

By August, Beck would stop his two weeks on/two weeks off rotation between his dad's house and our own. A schedule which started during asynchronous learning his freshman year. With him being home full-time, only traveling every other weekend to see his dad, we built a new sense of home, one which amassed board games to play during family night and attempted to find the right balance between group activities and needed moments of solitude. Beck's first day of school was celebrated with his choice in takeout and an ice cream cake. Over dinner, D tells Beck he's glad he's here. I agree, nodding maybe a little too emphatically while chewing a piece of salmon nigiri. It was homecoming of our own, one that offered peace of mind after everything we had gone through to get him here.

Maybe a semblance of peace of mind is more accurate. Although I wasn't waking up to subconscious panic attacks every night, I still didn't know how to reacclimate to life before the pandemic, perhaps because the world that came before it also didn't offer a solid source of comfort. I still had anxiety, political parties still struggled to find a middle ground, my son still had to practice active shooter drills throughout the school years.

Neuroticisms would come unannounced during the least ideal moments, like when we dropped Beck off at a nearby residential lake so he could take homecoming photos with his group of friends. On the way, he'd tell us that he's going with a group of half a dozen or so girls, and one other guy. I picture a million parents with flashing cameras. Small talk about the weather and unlimited questions. *How long have you been in Columbia? What do you do? Why haven't we seen you before?* I dread them asking me over for a cocktail or maybe catching a college football game.

Beck notices my discomfort. Maybe it was my grasp on the steering wheel tightening or the speed of my voice, increasing with each question. He tells me not to worry. "Parents don't have to come." I'll hate myself for believing him, but I'll still give a silent thanks to the way teenagers can be quietly gracious in the moments that count.

Within the hour, he'll send photos while D and I eat Chinese takeout. The first photo is Beck in front of a line of girls in sparkling dresses—everyone mask-free and laughing. Each of the half dozen girls are laughing, their eyes watching Beck, who is bent toward the ground as if he's picking something out, or perhaps it's a dance move from TikTok. I'll never know. D and I will text back joking how they are all in love with him, but he'd tell us later they're all just friends. Another photo features Beck and the only other guy in their party. Beck is standing behind him, his arms around his friends, their hands folding into each other. At 6'1", my son is nearly half a foot taller. In the picture you can see some parents to the side, laughing at the pair. My son and his friend are laughing, too. Everyone is laughing! I imagine the person on the other side of the camera—who is probably the other kid's mom—laughing, too.

I wonder if I should have bit the bullet and stayed rather than caving to anxiety again. I try not to hold onto the feeling for too long, which doesn't take much effort when I look at the photo one more time. When I zoom on Beck's smile mid-laughter—wide, all-teeth—a breath of relief escapes my body. I hadn't realized how long I had been holding the air in.

*

I'm ambivalent about my home. When people hear *Missouri*, they often repeat the name with an emphatic and drawn-out *misery*. Those same people are often alarmed I don't have an accent, which I wouldn't even possess being a product of my Coloradan father and my Michigander mother. I picture the images that run through their heads when they think of Missouri: kissing cousins, *Winter's Bone*, meth trailers, low IQs. But I think of Ozarks back roads, the kind to get lost in not because of not knowing how to get back home but because even the Trump supporters will waive at you when you find yourself between county lines. I'll drive past them waiving back—smile big but tight—even though they'd bat several eyes at the beliefs I held beyond the country road. In moments like this, I almost forget how, if my partner was with me, he wouldn't feel safe. Homes are always complicated, but this was never D's home. "I'm just trying to not get shot while I'm here," he often tells me.

I worry about my son staying in Missouri, but I have to remember that this is Beck's home, too.

*

Our stomachs are in the early stages of digestion when I get the call from Beck. We're watching a nineties rom-com. My pick. It's fifteen to ten—too early to be picked up.

"Hey, Mom. Can you come pick me up?" His voice is low and calm on the other end, and I'm already unnerved before he says the next sentence: "Someone brought a gun to the dance."

*

D insists on driving after I ran out into the street without shoes, repeating how someone brought a gun and we had to go. We had to go. The phrase will be a refrain for the amount of time it takes us to get to the high school. With each stop light, each car we get stuck behind, seven minutes combusts into a million years.

I didn't know what to expect to see when we reached the high school. The teenagers running down the street, sparkling underneath streetlamps in their formalwear, didn't offer much reassurance. When we arrive, I'm surprised to see students still coming out in waves. Some are crying. Some are running. Some are walking toward the police cars on the other side of the road.

D parks beside two cops at Beck's usual pickup spot—a coffee shop across the street. Every weekday afternoon, I watch Beck cross when the pedestrian light signals it's safe. More than once, cars have sped up despite the group of teenagers ready to walk to the other side. Just last week, there was a truck the size of god who blew through the red light, black exhaust spitting into the students faces whenever the driver smashed their foot to accelerate, as if the cloud of smoke was left on purpose. Every time I'm in this parking lot, I think of how easy it would be for anyone's child to not make it to the other side of the road. Tonight, it's an idea I can't shake.

Two girls are crying in a squad car, their hands clenched around pink chiffon and black organza. I search for Beck in between the waves of teenagers, some of them looking for parents, others walking home as quickly as they can. My eyes move so fast I get dizzy and have to close them, and all I can hear is the cop telling the girls to please not shout. In the midst of the chaos, the world becomes real, full of life, but the images and noise don't blur into a singular looming buzz.

Instead, each person's face looks clear, as if in autofocus. Their crying and tears almost tangible in the streetlights.

"There he is," D says, and I open my eyes again to find Beck in the middle of the newest wave. He's standing at the other side of the crosswalk, holding a girl's hand. I think, "Who the fuck is that?" It's an absurd thought to have in the midst of the gun scare. I'm thankful I didn't ask the question out loud. Until D responds with, "I don't know."

When the pedestrian light gives them the go ahead, they begin to walk. I can't take my eyes off my son as he crosses the road. and mid-way through, he catches D and I in the car, gives us a sad wave with his free hand. Time has slowed, and he can't make it to the car fast enough.

When he does, he says he's okay. "And yes, I had a date but didn't want to tell you." I laugh too loud, exasperated. "I have to do some consoling," he adds, nodding toward a girl in a blue dress. She's standing in the middle of a group of girls twenty feet away. Their sequined gowns shimmer from the red and blue squad lights.

When Beck is out of reach again, D comments on how he's so grown in the middle of all of this.

All of this, I repeat the words to myself. I repeat them again and hate what the weight of the three words means. Only months before, *all of this* meant shelter-in-place orders and a year of begrudging homeschooling. Just earlier today *all of this* meant shopping in a mall for a black button up, irritated at his mom for reminding him they could have done this sooner.

Time moves slower the longer Beck consoles his date. I don't recognize her from any of the homecoming photos Beck had sent hours ago. Maybe she's a classmate or from a different friend group. There's a small part of me that feels intrusive from staring. With some reluctance, I convince myself to look away to give them some privacy.

Across the street, there is a lone boy underneath a painted school name. He's standing directly under the mascot—a naked Kewpie doll with its hands raised in the air, a single alfalfa-cowlick on its head. I think about how D calls them "The Fighting Babies," which isn't as funny in this context. I wonder who the boy is calling, picture his mother on the other end, frantic and shoeless.

I distract myself by trying to guess Beck's dates name in my head, but Alyssa, Nikki, and Ashley all feel too old, too Millennial. Courtney. Amanda. What do young names sound like? I feel as old as this night. When I get to Kari, D interrupts. "He's such an adult," D says, and I look over again to see Beck's hands on her arms. He's saying something to her—perhaps he's sorry and they can go out another time, maybe he's just telling her it's okay, they're safe now. He kisses her head, waives goodbye, and walks toward the car, staring at the ground.

When he finally gets inside, he slams the door. He starts yelling, his voice is low, almost guttural. "We were having such a nice night such a nice night, and some asshole had to ruin it." He hits his fist on the window. His tears come out fast and angry. He starts yelling about the pandemic, how they've been shut in for over a year. The more he speaks, the quicker his cadence and the higher his inflection comes out. "How are guns still in schools after all this? Why does this keep happening?" His voice cracks into a long, "Why?"

*

The lull of 2020 fueled heighten reactions from restless bodies told to stay at home. Resistance to soft-mask mandates. Revenge shopping over the holidays, despite a budding recession. The restless bodies prone to violence resulted in an increase in gun violence and domestic abuse. In 2021 there was also a rise in school shootings—more than a hundred cases compared to school shootings in 2018 and 2019. Between the pandemic and a shift in presidents, this peak in active shooters was put on the media back burner. Until the Oxford High School shooting left four students dead in late November, two months after Beck's homecoming. We would have been coming back from a Thanksgiving in DC when we first heard the news. It will leave me unshocked, yet quieted. I'll stare out the window, looking out at corn fields, my eyes flicking back and forth between grandiose trucks stops and infinite green mile markers. You grieve for the parents. You see yourself in each one. Did they run out into the street and get into their cars without shoes, leaving leftover moo sho pork and the tv running, unpaused?

What if tonight had turned out different? The thought makes me nauseous, and I have to close my eyes and listen to the low hum of our tires on the road.

*

An hour after picking up Beck, I'll receive an email from Beck's principal, written to dispel any rumors parents may have heard. The letter will promise how, within the hour, they've done a thorough investigation of the premises for each report filed. The words are clearly written in a rush, filled with typos and false security. The principal ends the email praising students for raising $27,000 for local charities, but disregards how that money could have been used for metal detectors or counseling sessions for students who "reported seeing a gun." *The Columbia Tribune* will post an article that same night saying the rumors were unsubstantiated, how they closed the dance early because of the disruption, as if the students in formalwear running down the streets hadn't closed the dance down themselves.

On Facebook, parents respond. "There are pictures of the gun floating around the internet." "You tell a hundred kids in a stampede that they made up seeing a gun." "My daughter jumped a fence in a gown just to get enough out of reach to call me to tell me she loves me." I read the comments in bed, trying to ease my mind after everything. I ask myself aloud, "How do you find gun rumors unsubstantiated in less than an hour?" D agrees. Before he turns out the lights, he adds, "If a kid did bring a gun tonight, I just hope they aren't Black."

As I try to drift asleep, I replay the ride back home again and again, how no one said a word, but somehow Beck's silence was louder than the rest. The vibrations from the concrete were particularly noticeable on this drive. Perhaps it was the impenetrable quiet, or maybe it was because I still wasn't wearing shoes. I remember the way I did a double take as we passed a girl walking in a black satin dress, matching heels dangling from her hands. Fifteen years ago, I wore a similar dress to my first homecoming, which had ended with a dance to Bryan Adams's "(Everything I Do) I Do It for You," and a modest kiss with a boy I wouldn't remember often. My thoughts move to wondering what Beck's homecoming may have looked like if a kid hadn't waved a gun in the air. Would he have finished the night slow-dancing to SZA or maybe Olivia Rodrigo. Perhaps he would have kissed his unnamed date in the shimmering sky-blue dress. Instead, it ended with her crying in his arms, the cop lights still on, his mother watching from the passenger seat twenty feet away as he kissed the girl's forehead. In the comfort of my bed, I can still hear him crying in the back seat, his tears replacing the silence. In my memory, the sound of his tears replaces the silence, filling the entire space of the car and spilling out into the world. I can't shake how he didn't hide the noise, how he didn't hide anything at all.

The last image I see before sleep is a snapshot of my family getting out of the car and walking toward the door. I am the last one there, but before I can even ask if there is anything I can do, Beck tells me he doesn't feel like talking. At the door, D fumbles for the keys several times before finding a solid grasp. Although we were finally back, it isn't the front door that offers haven. It was the small moment that came before it, when D reached for Beck and hugged him, a stilled frame of home. Together, their bodies fall into each other, and D's voice breaks as he emphasizes for a second time: "I'm so glad you are here."

Overkill

Narratively, it would have been overkill to add how, when leaving the homecoming dance, my partner backed into a cop car illegally parked behind us.

Praying to Lyra

The only astronomy course I took was in my undergrad—a summer class with weekly trips to the observatory if weather permitted. Nearly a decade later, I can only place constellations if the time is midsummer and my location is home. Each July, thick Ozarks heat clings to my skin, and Lyra watches me from the east. Each July, I hope its brightest star, Vega, can tell I'm shining stronger than I was last year's July. Or: I hope Vega thinks I'm not doing too bad this time around.

At the observatory that summer, the ancient professor would point to summer constellations with a laser, and students would follow a trail of beamed red outlining the imagined lines of Cygnus and Cassiopeia, Ursa Major and Minor. We formed around him—silent, heads tilted toward the sky—as we went from constellation to constellation, starting with my sacred Lyra. The ancient professor beamed red light along the constellation's edges. Orpheus's lyre thrown to the heavens. As a whole, we shifted our feet toward each new constellation, our heads tipping away from the east and toward Scorpius in the south, stopping halfway to trace lasered lines in the shape of a kite: Bootes, the Herdsman, complete with two hounds and a club. On his left foot sits Arcturus, a guardian of the bear. "The bear being Ursa Major," the ancient professor explained, and we tilted our heads to keep up with the red beam, toward the north.

Later that summer, I'd show my son each constellation, starting with Lyra. My finger outlining the lyre's body, taking shape in the form of a parallelogram. I'd tell Beck how, even though it's a small constellation, it has one of the brightest stars. What I'd never tell him: how, in a dream that summer, I sat on the edges of one side of the parallelogram, and Orpheus the other; how—when I yelled across the void—the words dissipated into the space between us. And I'd never mention the way I woke up grasping to remember the message. Besides, can you remember the structure of words and sentences in dreams?

I worried about my son growing older and forming the same anxieties. He was seven, so I figured I had time. And because I couldn't pray to anything else, I started praying to Lyra. I've never told anyone any of my prayers, even the simplest one: *Please don't let Beck be like me*. It's an anxiety I already knew the answer to, confirmed in every moment I recognized myself in him: how he titled his head toward the night sky, the way his eyebrows narrow when he learns something remarkable.

*

I never prayed whenever blankets of clouds hid the night sky. Perhaps it's because I need to see something fully to know it fully sees me back. Or maybe it's because, on clouded evenings, I'm forced to be present in the world in front of me, and, these days, the world around me feels alien. Lately, clouded evenings sound like this: a fraternity house down the street filled to the brim with too-drunk bros and scattered sirens, a woman yelling, a man yelling louder. Maybe I don't pray when the night sky is hidden above blankets of clouds because what's buried underneath is a city of the dead, catacombs of a world that could have been. In order to pray, perhaps I need the brightness of something bigger than what I have pretended to be.

A prayer to Lyra is a prayer for the scattered Orpheus. The words fall out of my mouth without a trace of sound, soft wisps creating some form of remembrance.

Sorry, Orpheus, for your mistake in looking back, I say as a woman.

But what I really mean to say is: *Sorry, Orpheus, for not knowing who I am yet. I would have turned back, too.*

Even before Lyra, my prayers always felt more like apologies.

Sorry, god, for being uncomfortable with myself, for not knowing who I am yet, I'd say as a girl. Perhaps I pray to summer constellations over a semblance of god because, if they could, the myths caught in the sky would tell me, *I understand*, and, to me, that feels more like forgiveness.

*

I started praying more last year, even when Lyra wasn't in view. I prayed on clouded nights, during the day, in the winter months when Vega was absent altogether.

The stars were hidden from sunlight whenever I received the voicemail from my son's school. My stomach dropped at the missed call, already knowing the recording was about to confirm that my simplest prayer hadn't been answered. The words grew hazy—something about a lack of color, the weight of anxiety, something about an alarming text a friend reported to the counselor.

*

It's snowing in Vermont now—thick flakes that take their time falling from a sky empty of color. I'm here for my graduation residency, but the ten days hardly feel congratulatory without Beck here because of school.

Over the phone, I tell him how I wish he could see the Vermont snow.

"See those fat flakes?" I joke, switching cameras so he can. His face lights up on the other side of the screen, laughing back the words *fat flakes*.

"Looks nice," he says. "Wish I could be there, too."

I smile *it's okay*.

What I don't mention: how the Vermont snow is a whiteness you could fade into, and, if you are quiet enough, no one would ever know you were there. I won't tell him how it's difficult for light to pass through snowflakes because of its translucence, its lack of color, nor will I mention how a new friend just explained why snow brings a particular quiet, the noise of the world folding into the space between those fat flakes. It's a kind of quiet all too familiar for a person carrying a particular kind of sadness, moments when our minds are filled to the brim with thick thoughts that can also absorb sound if you let yourself fade into it all.

A fact about snow I save to tell Beck later: BBC *Earth* taught me how there are many sides to a snowflake. Even though it's difficult for light to pass through, the colorlessness causes light to reflect off of its body, its multiple sides "scattering light in many directions, diffusing the entire color spectrum." In a whiteout, the whiteness of clouds layered with the whiteness of snow diffuses light so heavily a shadow can't exist.

Lyra will be gone for most of the snow, but Vega's light will peak through again in April, and, with it, we'll see some color. Another year where I'll trace its parallelogram, showing Beck the lyre's lines. Maybe he'll roll his eyes when I remind him: Even though it's a small constellation, it has one of the brightest stars. Perhaps he will entertain me, narrowing his eyebrows after an emphatic, "Really?"

Whatever his response, I'll laugh. Eventually he'll laugh, too. Under my breath I'll say a prayer—this time for Orpheus and ourselves, soft wisps of thanks scattering across the night sky, the words settling in the spaces between us.

Brave New World

It's the day before your eighteenth birthday, and we are playing GoldenEye. D and you are impressed with my muscle memory from 1997, a year I had to keep up with my brother on that same game. I tell them how Chad and I opted for cheat codes for paintball bullets, writing curse words full of color on the wall. D says that's so inventive. You say you'd never think of that, but I think you would have just a handful of years earlier, before you were so close to the cusp of adulthood. In my mind, everyone is a child writing curse words with paintballs on the wall, or maybe I only hope they are—or at least parts of them. Perhaps I'm just afraid I'm still that child, refusing to grow up.

Tomorrow, you will read *Brave New World* under the big tree that sits in a flood plain along backroads. It's an English assignment for your last year in high school, and all I can think about is my own senior year, when I came back to school two months after welcoming you into this world. Everyone kept telling me I was brave to have you, but it also felt loaded, like I was living one of their own dystopias and they were just trying to be polite.

Tomorrow, a contract for this book will be waiting in my inbox whenever I wake up. As someone inclined toward subtle metaphor, the symbolism feels a little too obvious for it to be true, but I'll wake up, and the contract is there. I'm so overcome with emotion that I miss the connection, the obvious timing of it all. I'm already in bits and pieces from you becoming an adult, still holding onto an image of my hands pressing headphones to my belly, Beethoven's sonatas seeping out the foam. Or the image of the quiet morning drive to the hospital, a nurse at the front desk telling me she had a baby young too, and things can turn out all right.

Thank You for Staying with Me

"Isn't Clark such a rider?" my mom asks. "He's such a good rider." Ten seconds before she was yelling at him to get off the center console.

We're driving from Missouri to Oregon with her seventy-pound retriever mix in the back seat. Clark is not a very good rider, but I'll hear my mom convince him otherwise for the next thirty hours. He'll respond by standing between us, his hot breath filling my mom's hybrid Ford Fusion.

She says she's grateful I'm able to take this trip with her. She tears up before she finishes her sentence. We've already made it through the Badlands, across Wyoming and Montana. I ask her if she wants to go to the John Day Fossil Beds when we get closer to my brother's house, where she'll spending the next few years watching over his newborn daughter, reading her books in a room decorated in painted octopuses and a mobile with flying narwhals.

A stuffed octopus from the Georgia Aquarium sits in the backseat. I bought it on the way back from D's mother's funeral three months before. Amelia was born two days after Dorothy died. At the aquarium, I picked up the stuffed animal in the gift shop with my brother's nursery theme in mind—not "ocean life," but "narwhals and octopuses," specifically. Holding the octopus in the checkout line, I asked D if it was hard to celebrate life so soon after the biggest death. He said no, not at all. He thought it was a beautiful thing, and I do my best not to cry. In my mind, I name the octopus Dot, a name his mother was often called but I never knew how to call her. It feels like a way of introducing D's mother to my family, even though no one will ever know it.

I show my mother a picture of the fossil beds which is about five hours outside of our final destination in McMinnville.

"Ooh, pretty. I'm up for it. I'll try anything," she says. "Except for anal." She smiles to herself. I smile, too, trying not to think about how she won't be making the drive back with me. I don't know how to tell her that I already miss her dirty jokes, that I already miss her. She will make the anal joke thirty more times, and I'll never grow sick of it.

*

We make it to Idaho without listening to music. I'll struggle to remember the brunt of our conversations that took the place of our go-tos — Cat Stevens, Ben Folds, fucking Yanni. At first only jokes about anal and telling Clark he's such a good boy surface in my memory. Talks that will come up later, bit by bit: how Missouri has often meant loneliness for my mother, but she'll still miss her little bungalow — the first place she felt like home after my dad left over twenty years ago; how she's so happy Chad and I have found partners who make it a point to stay.

I'll remember we talked about the changing landscapes as we drove further west, how one cloud looked phallic for a moment, but the wind kept pushing it up and outward, so the erection got too out of hand. I remember looking for shops along the way to find matching stone rings, but we were always too late or too far away. I don't tell my mom I had spent the quiet moments considering what stone would be best for the two of us, a mother and a daughter saying goodbye. I won't tell her I'm worried I won't know what home will feel like without her.

*

The days blur together when we finally get to Oregon. On our last day, my mom wants to take me to the coast. I tell her I feel torn — I've hardly spent time with the rest of the family while I've been here. But she looks hurt, her eyes always on the verge of tears, and guilt washes over me. I tell her, Okay, let's go. I say, "It'll be fun."

She smiles, satisfied. "I just wanted to watch the sea lions with you." She reminds me of how I wanted to be a marine biologist as a little girl.

"You could name all the whales by heart." I feel like a small girl again, and suddenly the thought of our last day together rips me inside out.

When she sees my eyes water over, she says, "Don't you do it." She wipes away her own tear, adding, "If you cry, I'll cry. And I'm not sure I'll know how to stop."

The drive to the coast takes an hour. Our first stop is in Tillamook, where Clark and her will be living with family friend. Inside, she shows me her cozy basement apartment and the porch table where she'll do puzzles. *She's always wanted a table just for puzzles.* By the end of the tour, I know where her bed will be, the places where she thought her bed could be, where she'll put her recliner and another chair for a guest. She isn't sure where she'll put the TV, but she will figure it out later. She says there aren't many options. For the entirety of the tour, I'm ambivalent. The way my mother talks about her new space is endearing, and while I know this move offers healing, I can already feel the loaded sadness in our unsaid goodbyes. There's a growing nervousness that comes with her getting older, moving up and down the stairs to the new space she calls home.

The drive from Tillamook to Newport offers peace. The state highway winds between tall woods and the Pacific. There's a calm here that can't be found in any part of Missouri I've seen—even the rivers and the edges of the Ozark mountains on my favorite back roads drive.

We pass through a town named Beaver, which makes my mom and I laugh forever. "I wonder if a gynecologist works here," she says through her laughter, punctuating the joke with: "Beaver Gynecology!" Even though the town only lasts for a handful of heartbeats, I still find myself disappointed Beaver doesn't offer any OBGYN services. I see a Volkswagen auto shop and a store that sells both groceries and firearms. *Maybe we aren't that far from Missouri.* It's a thought that's dark but makes me breathe easier.

As soon as she said "Beaver Gynecology," I thought of the white walls of the delivery room the day Beck was born. Nurses hovering over me, asking if I could feel the epidural yet. My mom had gone out to lunch when I was dilated at a six. By the end of lunch, I was at a ten, and everyone in the world was asking if I was ready. How could I be ready when my mother was out to lunch? One nurse handed me a phone, asked me to call her, but between the numbness of the anesthesia and knowing that everything was about to change, I had forgotten the numbers, mixing the fours with the sixes. I looked up, hopeless.

"It's okay, it happens all the time," the nurse said. Perhaps she knew I just needed my mother, that some universality in forgetting would make me feel like every other grown woman. She was the same nurse who, at the beginning of the day, told me she also had a baby at seventeen. "It'll be okay," she told me, moving her hand as if to say, *ta-daaa*. Normally the gesture would feel patronizing, but I didn't have any energy left to analyze her intention. I was in a wheelchair with nowhere to go but down the hall, overcome what was coming next.

My mother returned right before I had to push and was irritated the labor only took twenty minutes. "You took thirty-six hours to get out of me. Stubborn from the start."

*

"I wanted to take you to this restaurant for a long time," my mom says to me as we park. "You can see the boats come and go. If you're lucky, you'll catch the sea lions swimming between the docks." In my periphery, I know she's watching me stare out the window. I can see her smile, too. "I knew you'd love it," she says.

I do love it, but that's not what I'm thinking. I'm wondering which one of her recent trips to Oregon she ate here. The bitter part of me guesses it was the time my brother surprised her with a trip for Mother's Day four months ago. It was supposed to be her last Mother's Day in Missouri, but she wasn't fazed by my lack of excitement for her trip—couldn't read my dead-pan tone when I said, "How neat." I'm trying to learn how to let these things go, reminding myself I can sometimes be too sensitive. Maybe I wouldn't have been so hurt if it wasn't the ocean she was visiting.

We make a game, ordering cocktails with the weirdest names, like Eeyore's Requiem or Stormwatching Weather. She wanted to come early to avoid the crowds, but we ended up being the only ones in the restaurant for the better part of an hour. We fill the space with laughter and seaport observations.

Everything in Oregon is more expensive, which is easy to get away with when the seafood is fresh, the drink names are quirky, and there is no sales tax. She tells me not to worry about money when she catches me raising my eyebrows at the prices of Brazilian stew and Dungeness crab soup. "I'll cover it," she says, and I'm both relieved and worried. The sale of her bungalow just went through, but that money is all she has besides the cash she'll get from babysitting a couple of times a week. It'll be another few months before she's sixty-five and qualifies for Social Security.

In between Eeyore's Requiems, we watch the boats come in. She points at the closest dock, says "Look at that sea lion. Watch her go down." I see a sea lion's head bobbing above the water just before dunking her face underneath to look for fish. The sea lion disappears for a few seconds, and my mom makes another game of guessing where she'll pop up next: by the rocky shore, by the other side of the pier, by the boat that looks forgotten. We guess incorrectly every time, but that feels more entertaining than always being right.

The table tent highlights seasonal drinks and plates for the fall. Smokey the Pear Sour and Blood Orange Sidecar. Creamy miso tuna and a returning seasonal favorite: an oyster and spinach salad. I want everything. The freshest seafood in Missouri is crawdads or trout or a variety of sad-mouthed catfish. The other side of the tent features a photo of a Dungeness crab and the crustacean's local history. I read about Newport being the Dungeness Crab Capital of the World, accounting for a third of the capital in the state's fisheries. I think about ecdysis, the way crabs molt their hard shells as they get older to make room for new growth.

My mother interrupts my reading: "I knew it was time to move because I could feel everything was going to be okay. And Beck was going to be okay, too." She pauses, says everything again, and we cry.

*

Mother sea lions have a special call for their pups, a sequence so unique, only the two of them will understand. When coming back to her rookery, a mother will make this call—a whining trumpet—as she looks for her child. Wading through the sea of basking lions, she'll keep calling, listening for her pup, who makes its own bleating cry in response to its mother.

My own mother starts every birthday singing Happy Birthday in the form of sea lion barks—a special call only her pups will understand. Until this year, my brother and I had always thought she was imitating a dog until she corrected me when I turned thirty-three. She called and sang Happy Birthday with actual human words. At the end I laughed, said thank you. "But why didn't you bark like a dog?" There's a part of me that worries it's because I'm too old or that she had failed to remember the tradition.

She was offended I had gotten it wrong my whole life. "A dog?" she says, exasperated. "I was barking like a seal!"

Seals don't bark, they're more of a grunting and tongue-clicking vibe, but I didn't correct her. Instead, I just told her I missed the Happy Birthday barks, and she promised me she'd do it next year. I tried not to think about how we'd be two thousand miles away when I turn thirty-four—if the states separating us would make barking "Happy Birthday," whether dog or sea lion, feel more distant.

*

A package the size of several baby seals arrives two days before Christmas. On the phone, my mom tells me half of the items are three stockings. "Not actual stockings," she says. "I put everything in Christmas wine sleeves."

My wine sleeve is decorated with a Santa who looks a little drunk but very happy and contains her Christmas staples: a Toblerone bar, a pack of gum, beef jerky, smoked oysters, a clementine for good luck. Our usual Slim Jim's were absent, replaced with beef jerky from a specialty store in Tillamook. The can of smoked oysters is from a fish market just down the coast, somewhere between her new home and Newport.

At the bottom is a small stone, I can tell by the smooth polish and its weight in my hands—I can tell by the hundreds of stones I've held throughout my life. I smile to myself, my hand still closed. I can hear her say, "I know how much you love a good rock."

Then my brother, the geophysicist, correcting her: "It's a mineral."

While D and Beck comment on their own wine sleeve stocking gifts, I close my eyes and take guesses at what stone it could be. Perhaps something the color of the ocean. Sodalite or azurite. It's a game my mom and I used to play when I was a child. I only had a handful of stones then, so the game was much easier. If it had rough edges it was fool's gold. If it was a polished stone the size of a half dollar, I knew it was my favorite—a malachite swirling with layered orbs of greens my mom and I called small planets.

This stone doesn't have an organic shape though. It's carved. I open my hand and my eyes and see a small sea lion—green and pink—in the palm of my hand. Unakite, a stone for grounding and rebirth.

*

On the drive to Oregon, my mother told me something I never knew.

"I didn't want you to have an abortion because I knew a girl who had one, and even though it was the right choice for her, it still weighs her down, almost fifty years later."

I asked her why she didn't just tell me that? And she breathes in and lets out small yelp.

"The way you feel everything . . . I just didn't want you to carry that with you forever,"

For sixteen years, I thought she was trying to sway me under the guise of religion—a resentment that has waned, but I struggled to let go of. I never thought it could be borne out of love. Then, in a handful of words, everything evaporated—flew out the window or into Clark's mouth as he panted between us, his front paws pressing into the center console.

"I was just so scared for you." The words hang between us, replacing a wall built in conjunction. The words are still there days later, sitting with us at my brother's kitchen table. The tears were already halfway down her face by the time I said it's time for me to go.

"I've been dreading this moment," she said, and I tell her I know — *me too*. Her hair smelled like a combination of Lake Michigan and the discontinued perfume she wore in the nineties. It's the scent of a distant kind of motherhood.

She breathed in a sob, not letting herself release fully.

"I'll see you soon enough," I tell her. My words start out strong, but by the end of the sentence, they come out in a low, wavering cry. The sound of a bleating pup. What I meant to say was: *Thank you for staying with me when I didn't know how to be. I'll be alright now. I'll be okay.*

ACKNOWLEDGMENTS

Endless gratitude to Courtney Ochsner at the University of Nebraska Press. It was terrifying submitting this book—this raw nerve—to a stranger, and you made the process so easy on me. I'm not sure I'd have the courage to put this book out into the world if it hadn't been for you.

This manuscript wouldn't have been the same without thoughtful copyedits from Anne McPeak. I could have cried throughout this entire process, and her patience and knowledge saved my life.

I've fangirled over every single person who wrote a blurb for this book, and I'm still in disbelief that you all agreed to take the time to read my work: Matthew Gavin Frank, Jennifer Maritza McCauley, Phong Nguyen, Abigail Thomas, Sue William Silverman, and Kathy Fish.

My writing journey is filled with mentors who continuously influenced me in their own creative works and pedagogical values, starting with my seventh-grade English teacher, Priscilla Arens, who was one of the first people I told I was pregnant at seventeen. She was also the first person to tell me I was going to be a writer. Jack Knight and Daniel Kaufman made philosophy classes interesting enough that I didn't drop out my undergraduate year. Michael Czyzniejewski and Jen Murvin were my first writing mentors who made me want to write well, and since then, Trinie Dalton, Harrison Candelaria Fletcher, Barbara Hurd, Trudy Lewis, Patrick Madden, Phong Nguyen, Nance Van Winckel, Julija Šukys, and Robert Vivian have all shaped how I write, and in turn, how I navigate the world.

I wouldn't have been able to finish this collection without the guidance of Sue William Silverman, a mentor who may have quite literally saved me from myself. Her continuous support made me want to support others in their own writing journeys.

I've been blessed with a long list of friends throughout this life. While the list is too long to name you all, I'm forever grateful to those who have pushed me and my work forward, whether through writing together or just staying with me through a hard time: Elizabeth Austin, Gideon Belin, Nikki Boss, Jason and Renee Brown, Katie Brown, Rowan Buckton, Natalie Byers, Michelle Campbell, Joel Coeltharp, Jesse Cornea, Sarah Curtis, Brenna Douglas, Caylin Capra-Thomas, Amanda Futrell, Grae Gardiner, Amanda Hadlock, Andrew Hahn, Jacob Hall, AnnElise Hatjakes, Tay Lorenzo, Hannah Major, Cassidy McCants, Miriam McEwan, Jas McMullen, Eric Morris-Pusey, Shane Page, Rima Rantisi, Genevieve Richards, John Robertson, Sierra Sitzes, Kella Thornton, Kali VanBaale, and Abby Webster.

Thank you to the Stoop Kids. I think of Stoop memories, saturated in the Vermont snow almost every day.

Thank you to Norm MacDonald's Book Club 1.0. I hated reading Anna Karenina so many times, but you all made me appreciate reading before college literature courses.

Maa and Gramps, Norm, Dorothy Quist, Guarra Shekhar, Ernie Hadley, Thom Thom: I wish you were here on this plane of existence so I could hug you once more and thank you in person. I miss you with all of my being. I hope you are out there, somewhere, whatever that means.

I'm forever thankful for my disjointed-but-fiercely-loving families, in particular my brother, who told me to stop talking about what I wanted to do and just do it—advice that convinced me to return to school during a time when I wasn't sure I was capable of anything.

And to my mother: Thank you for this world. I'm sorry it took us so long to get here, but I'm grateful you possessed the courage for these essays to be written, even though they were a lot to take in. It was a process that helped me understand just how scary it is to be a mother, especially a mother of a strong-willed daughter.

    This book couldn't exist without Donald Quist and Beck, who gave me a home when I couldn't remember what home looked like. I love this little family we've made, a family where we can talk about art and life and hopes and fears and the future, knowing each person is listening with care. Thank you for this life, for this timeline. Thank you for all of this.

Thanks to the editors of the journals where these essays were first published:

> *Willow Springs Magazine*: "Second Molars"
>
> *Doubleback Review*: "Wall of Water"
>
> *Past Ten*: "Unbreaking the Egg," originally published as "September 4th, 2009"
>
> *Hayden's Ferry Review*: "A Scattering of Our Own"
>
> *Wigleaf*: "Matted and Mangled"
>
> *Hobart* and HAD: "If You Build It, Baseball Dads will Come"
>
> *Writing in the Dark*: "Reclaiming Voices Like Needles in Haystacks"
>
> AGNI: "D Explains How to Speak to a Police Officer," originally published as a cowritten piece with Donald Quist titled "How to Speak to a Police Officer"
>
> *No Contact Magazine*: "All Things Being Equal"
>
> *Apple in the Dark Magazine*: "Praying to Lyra"

IN THE AMERICAN LIVES SERIES

The Twenty-Seventh Letter of the Alphabet: A Memoir
by Kim Adrian

Fault Line
by Laurie Alberts

Pieces from Life's Crazy Quilt
by Marvin V. Arnett

Songs from the Black Chair: A Memoir of Mental Interiors
by Charles Barber

This Is Not the Ivy League: A Memoir
by Mary Clearman Blew

Body Geographic
by Barrie Jean Borich

Driving with Dvořák: Essays on Memory and Identity
by Fleda Brown

Searching for Tamsen Donner
by Gabrielle Burton

Island of Bones: Essays
by Joy Castro

American Lives: A Reader
edited by Alicia Christensen
introduced by Tobias Wolff

If This Were Fiction: A Love Story in Essays
by Jill Christman

Get Me Through Tomorrow: A Sister's Memoir of Brain Injury and Revival
by Mojie Crigler

Tell Me about Your Bad Guys: Fathering in Anxious Times
by Michael Dowdy

Should I Still Wish: A Memoir
by John W. Evans

Out of Joint: A Private and Public Story of Arthritis
by Mary Felstiner

Descanso for My Father: Fragments of a Life
by Harrison Candelaria Fletcher

Homing: Instincts of a Rustbelt Feminist
by Sherrie Flick

My Wife Wants You to Know I'm Happily Married
by Joey Franklin

Weeds: A Farm Daughter's Lament
by Evelyn I. Funda

Autumn Song: Essays on Absence
by Patrice Gopo

Shift: A Memoir of Identity and Other Illusions
by Penny Guisinger

Falling Room
by Eli Hastings

It's Fun to Be a Person I Don't Know
by Chachi D. Hauser

Borderline Citizen: Dispatches from the Outskirts of Nationhood
by Robin Hemley

The Distance Between: A Memoir
by Timothy J. Hillegonds

Opa Nobody
by Sonya Huber

Pain Woman Takes Your Keys, and Other Essays from a Nervous System
by Sonya Huber

Hannah and the Mountain: Notes toward a Wilderness Fatherhood
by Jonathan Johnson

Under My Bed and Other Essays
by Jody Keisner

Local Wonders: Seasons in the Bohemian Alps
by Ted Kooser

A Certain Loneliness: A Memoir
by Sandra Gail Lambert

Bigger than Life: A Murder, a Memoir
by Dinah Lenney

What Becomes You
by Aaron Raz Link and Hilda Raz

Queen of the Fall: A Memoir of Girls and Goddesses
by Sonja Livingston

The Virgin of Prince Street: Expeditions into Devotion
by Sonja Livingston

Anything Will Be Easy after This: A Western Identity Crisis
by Bethany Maile

Such a Life
by Lee Martin

Turning Bones
by Lee Martin

In Rooms of Memory: Essays
by Hilary Masters

Island in the City: A Memoir
by Micah McCrary

Thank You for Staying with Me: Essays
by Bailey Gaylin Moore

Between Panic and Desire
by Dinty W. Moore

To Hell with It: Of Sin and Sex, Chicken Wings, and Dante's Entirely Ridiculous, Needlessly Guilt-Inducing Inferno
by Dinty W. Moore

Let Me Count the Ways: A Memoir
by Tomás Q. Morín

Shadow Migration: Mapping a Life
by Suzanne Ohlmann

Meander Belt: Family, Loss, and Coming of Age in the Working-Class South
by M. Randal O'Wain

Sleep in Me
by Jon Pineda

The Solace of Stones: Finding a Way through Wilderness
by Julie Riddle

Works Cited: An Alphabetical Odyssey of Mayhem and Misbehavior
by Brandon R. Schrand

Thoughts from a Queen-Sized Bed
by Mimi Schwartz

My Ruby Slippers: The Road Back to Kansas
by Tracy Seeley

The Fortune Teller's Kiss
by Brenda Serotte

Gang of One: Memoirs of a Red Guard
by Fan Shen

Just Breathe Normally
by Peggy Shumaker

How to Survive Death and Other Inconveniences
by Sue William Silverman

The Pat Boone Fan Club: My Life as a White Anglo-Saxon Jew
by Sue William Silverman

Scraping By in the Big Eighties
by Natalia Rachel Singer

Sky Songs: Meditations on Loving a Broken World
by Jennifer Sinor

In the Shadow of Memory
by Floyd Skloot

Secret Frequencies: A New York Education
by John Skoyles

The Days Are Gods
by Liz Stephens

Phantom Limb
by Janet Sternburg

This Jade World
by Ira Sukrungruang

The Sound of Undoing: A Memoir in Essays
by Paige Towers

When We Were Ghouls:
A Memoir of Ghost Stories
by Amy E. Wallen

Knocked Down: A High-Risk Memoir
by Aileen Weintraub

Yellowstone Autumn: A Season of
Discovery in a Wondrous Land
by W. D. Wetherell

This Fish Is Fowl: Essays of Being
by Xu Xi

To order or obtain more information on these or other University of Nebraska Press titles, visit nebraskapress.unl.edu.

www.ingramcontent.com/pod-product-compliance
Lightning Source LLC
Chambersburg PA
CBHW061520040325
22904CB00016B/75